Wayne McLennan was born in Ne   1954. He now lives with his wife   business in Estonia. His previous bc   ...ska was published by Granta Books.

Also by Wayne McLennan

Rowing to Alaska – and Other True Stories

TENT BOXING

An Australian Journey

WAYNE McLENNAN

Granta Books

London

Granta Publications, 2/3 Hanover Yard, Noel Road, London N1 8BE

First published in Great Britain by Granta Books 2007

Copyright © Wayne McLennan, 2007

Wayne McLennan has asserted his moral right under the
Copyright, Designs and Patents Act, 1988, to be identified as
the author of this work.

All rights reserved. No reproduction, copy or transmissions
of this publication may be made without written
permission. No paragraph of this publication may be
reproduced, copied or transmitted save with written
permission or in accordance with the provisions of the
Copyright Act 1956 (as amended). Any person who does
any unauthorized act in relation to this publication may be
liable to criminal prosecution and civil claims for damages.

A CIP catalogue record for this book is available
from the British Library.

1 3 5 7 9 10 8 6 4 2

ISBN 13: 978-1-86207-854-3
ISBN 10: 1-86207-854-8

Typeset by M Rules

Printed and bound in Great Britain by William Clowes Ltd, Beccles, Suffolk

For my darling sister, Michelle Geale (1972-2006), as brave as they come.

CONTENTS

'Now, whoever has courage and a strong and collected spirit in his breast, let him come forward, lace on the gloves and put up his hands.'

VIRGIL

INTRODUCTION

It was the jerky movements of the crumpled, wispy old man sitting across from me that caught my attention. His face, although blotched, deeply creased and peeling from years of exposure to scorching suns, still had an impish youthfulness. When I paid more attention to the hands, which moved constantly, I could see that the skin was paper thin and criss-crossed with stringy azure veins, and that his fingers were browned on the end as if they had been roasted in an oven and basted from time to time like a Sunday roast dinner. I knew then that he was a smoker, and that he badly needed a smoke.

When he noticed me looking, a nervous grin broke across his face, one eye closed, and his head twisted in that strange way that many Australians have of acknowledging you physically before greeting you with words. 'How ya going, mate?' he finally said. 'Dry, ain't it?'

And so we settled into each other's company, drifting in and out of conversation, sticking with subjects that were comfortable, neutral; the weather, how bad the bloody government was, how the whole country was going to hell, while the bus moved along smoothly, steadily.

Sometimes the old man would doze, and then I was happy that

he was spared for a few moments the torment of not being able to light his smoke. During those times, which became more frequent as the bus moved ever steadily westward, deeper into the NSW bush, I would glance out of the window, taking in the country, my country that I had left more than twenty-five years ago.

On the first part of our journey, our bus passed shaded, rambling houses perched on hills that overlooked large green paddocks hedged in with paling-fences and filled with thorough-breds. I knew these were horse studs, and I envied my country and the luck that some people have in their lives, and again felt the old sadness that I carried with me of a man who has left paradise.

When we crossed a rocky range, leaving behind the valley that the Hunter River watered, the horses were gone. Cattle and sheep picked at pale, meagre grass. Eucalyptus trees with bark the texture of leather, and leaves faded to grey and brittle as chalk, dotted the undulating country with the distant horizons. Once, far off, I saw a line of green coolabahs rooted by a river, but the thin watercourse, as if ashamed that it could help so little wound away into the distance, and then it was gone.

'Dry ain't it, mate?' the old man repeated for the umpteenth time, as if that were the first thought in people's heads, and when there was nothing else to say, there was always that. I only nodded, because it was not really a question, it was the way it was.

'What are you heading out west for anyway?'

'I'm going to join a boxing troupe,' I answered, happy that he was awake, intimidated by the hardness outside the window, and the uncertainty of my future.

'I thought that wasn't allowed any more?' he asked, reaching into a soiled plastic sport bag on the seat next to him, freeing a Thermos and pouring black tea into the Thermos cup that he sipped before handing it to me.

'They're taking the tent up to Queensland, it's still legal up there.'

'Umm,' he murmured, 'them buggers up there ud let you do anything if you had the money to pay. You look a little old though, mate,' he added, after taking back the proffered tea that was now half empty and slurping loudly.

'I don't plan on fighting,' I answered.

He nodded thoughtfully, 'I fought in the boxing tent once!'

The old man then scratched at an itch on the back of his head, and looked towards the ceiling of the bus as if the memory of that fight was etched in the roof above him.

'It was forty-eight, just after the war. I was wandering around the Royal Easter with me mates, we were all working on the wharfs in Sydney at the time. Gee, it was hard work, but the wages were good. Fit as Mallee bulls we were. Anyway, we ran up against this crowd, and it was so thick, you couldn't get through. We knew straight away it was Sharman's boxing tent all right.' The old man then took a deep breath, as if drawing on a cigarette, before adding, 'There were a lot around in those days, but Sharman's always had the Royal Easter.

'A fella wearing a white shirt and tie was up on the board spruiking away,' the man continued, his voice quickening. 'He had all his boxers lined up either side of him, all dressed in gowns and boxing boots; there must have been fifteen of them, mostly Aboriginal boys if I remember rightly. And then he said that if any fella wanted to have a go, all he had to do was put up his hand.

'I'm standing there with my mates, minding my own business, listening to this bloke, not thinking of being so bloody stupid, and then the drum starts, boom ba-boom ba-boom.'

The old man's lips barely opened as he made the drum sound, his pale stained hand tapped on the armrest, each tap growing heavier as the sounds in his memory grew stronger.

'And then they started ringing this big brass bell, keeping the same rhythm as the drum, and I suppose it was more than I could take, because next thing I know, I'm standing there with my hand in the air like a bloody school kid who knows the answer. And this bloke's saying, come up here young fella, let that young fella through.'

The bus passed a shrunken watering dam. Sheep, heavy and ungainly in their matted coats of winter wool, stood unsteadily on the hard rough crust of mud at the water's edge, slurping at the brown liquid. And then we passed another, and another.

'Well, I couldn't turn back then, could I, so I pushed through the crowd as cocky as I could manage, climbed the ladder and stood on the board next to one of the tent fighters.

The old man hesitated a moment, deciding something. 'Well, I'll tell you the truth, my legs were shaking like a bloody leaf when I was standing up there, but then the fella in the white shirt and tie had a word to me, asked me a few questions about myself, and introduced me to the crowd. Then he matched me up against one of his fighters, a young Aboriginal fella with a big flat nose, and then the boom ba boom ba boom started again, and I felt all right.'

'How'd ya go?' I asked, but the old man seemed not to hear the question, as he struggled with the decorated lid of a round, shiny tin. His nails, bitten short, couldn't grab a hold on the rim. When he finally prised it open, I could see that it was filled with dark stringy tobacco, and lying on top of the tobacco was a sheath of snow white papers.

'Nearly there,' he said, as he shaped the strong smelling weed in the palm of his hand, before tipping it into a cigarette paper.

'I didn't know they still sold those tins any more.'

'I bought it at a market, it's original all right, but I just fill it up with this packet tobacco,' the old man answered, before making a final roll of the paper between his fingers, dragging his tongue along the gummy edge and sealing it shut.

'Well,' I said again, 'how did you go?'

The old man smiled, showing off a mouthful of pearly white plastic teeth. 'The first round I think he must have been taking it a bit easy with me, because I thought I was doing pretty good, but when I gave him a hard smack in the mouth, he just walloped me all over the ring. I lasted the fight though. Don't know how.'

'Were you sorry you fought?'

'Sorry . . . no. Look, mate, there I was, an eighteen-year-old kid, standing on Jimmy Sharman's line-up board amongst some of the best young fighters around and with the beat of that drum running through my body. Behind me there was this canvas mural of Darcy, Henneberry, Richards, Tommy Burns, and you know them boys were our best boxers, and they had all fought in the tent. And the crowd, the ones who never had the guts to get up, were standing there looking up at me and clapping because I did get up. After the fight, my mates never stopped buying me beer, and till the time I left Sydney, I was known at work as the fella who fought in the tent. And all it cost me was a few bruises and a bloody nose.'

The bus stopped at a town built amongst rolling hills, and the old man grabbed his sports bag and pulled himself stiffly up and out of his seat, his cigarette set firmly in his mouth ready for lighting as soon as he left the bus.

'See ya later, mate, thanks for the yarn,' he said as he passed. Then he stopped and turned slowly back to me. 'You'll fight, mate. You won't be able to help it.' And then I waved him goodbye.

An hour later the bus, almost empty, rolled into Dubbo train station, the last stop on its journey from the coast. I got off, collected my bag and swag from the driver, and squatted by the kerb, waiting to be picked up by a man I'd never met.

Aboriginal families surrounded by great mounds of baggage waited patiently for trains that would take them further into the bush, or back to Sydney's distraught inner suburb of Redfern, where so many had made their home amongst the strangers from different tribes.

Their children ran about frantically, effortlessly, using the concrete of the station platforms as football fields and play-grounds. The young ones screamed unrestrained; piercing, joyous. A midday drunk, an Aboriginal, staggered by, noticed me, but could not seem to focus, wiped at his nose with the back of his sleeve, gave up any thought that he could profit from me, and moved into the comradeship of his mates who huddled around a bottle, sipping secretly. The sky was cloudless; it had been for months.

It had been half a lifetime since I had taken any sort of work in Australia. I had become a middle-aged man, and I needed to find back my country before it was too late: moving constantly during adult life had rendered me tribeless. To certain people that can be a liberation, to me it was crippling. It was time I came home.

I had thought that the era of travelling boxing tents had passed. The last time I had been inside one was in 1969; it had been in Cessnock, my hometown in the coalfields of NSW. When I remembered that night, it was always with a warm sense of nostalgia. I could recall with unnatural clarity some of the boxers lined up on the board in front of the banners. I could sense the excitement and apprehension amongst the men and boys who milled together outside the tent listening to the spruiker describe the history and circumstances of his boxers, praising their talents, and then, encouraging and finally haranguing the crowd to take the chance and fight one of his men for money. And I remembered that in Cessnock, he always found willing takers.

The tent was an important feature of the sideshows that travelled from town to town as a part of the Agricultural Show, and the Agricultural Show was the most important event in the calendar year of our town; of all country towns. For the miners and sons of miners of Cessnock, the boxing tent was our greatest play house, a place were local legends could be born; certainly small and insignificant in the eyes of most people, but nevertheless, in the often uneventful life of working man, these legends had substance and were often carried through till the end. For some of us it was still more: to fight in the tent was our initiation into manhood.

The boxing tent never returned to Cessnock after 1969. State governments enacted new laws, which ordered that tent boxers had to suffer under the same rules as professional boxers; that is, not fight more than once a week, and also, that a doctor had to be in attendance. Tent boxers had been known to fight seventeen times in one day, and they would have scoffed at the idea of having a doctor in tow. It was economically impossible for tent boxing to continue and so sixty odd years of tradition ended. But Australians have always been plagued by politicians who constantly need to create new laws, marking out their territory like a dog pissing on trees.

I felt it very personally because I never fought in the boxing tent. In 1969 I was fifteen, too young or too fearful. We all have our great personal regrets, and not fighting in the tent lingered as one of mine. I went on to fight successfully as an amateur boxer, and much less successfully as a professional, but it still haunted me.

By chance, I discovered that boxing tents were still travelling through Queensland. A beer, a yarn with an old fighter in a pub in

Sydney; a recollection. My research led me to an article written in 1988 about Bells Touring Boxing Troupe. I knew it was a tent with history and tradition, one that had been around from the beginning.

The present owner was Michael John Karaitiana, grandson of Roy Bell, the man who started up the boxing tent at the beginning of the depression years. I called Michael in his home in Tullamore, in the bush of NSW, and I asked him if he would take me along on his next boxing run. I told him I would earn my keep as good as anybody.

Michael had a deep Australian accent and like most Antipodeans, an easy direct way of talking. A prince or a pauper, it was all the same to him. He would call me consistently in the middle of the night, unaware that there was a time difference between Australia and Europe, that I had already been asleep for hours.

I wondered at first whether he cared that he kept waking me up, but after the shortest time I knew that there was no inconsideration meant, there was too much geniality and sincerity. It was like sitting with a mate in the pub only you were still in your pyjamas. The details of time were not important to him. I knew I could have called him night or day without fear of retribution.

And I did call him many times. When his wife answered it was always with extreme politeness, but with a detachment, as if she never really believed that I was coming, or that Michael would take the tent on the road. Often he was not there. 'Cleaning up the dump,' I would be told, or building a shed, or a fence, or hauling wheat.

Sometimes I was left thinking, I thought he was a boxing tent owner. One time I asked him about all the different jobs, and he admitted that he hadn't taken the tent on the road for years, and did whatever needed to be done to feed his family.

And there were the children. How many I couldn't tell, but

voices of different ages would answer when I called, and then I would hear 'Dad, it's that man again,' or sometimes, just a cute 'Daddy.' It was never sure until the last phone call whether Michael would travel or not. Slowly, I began to understand his wife's reserve.

The biggest problem, Michael explained to me once, was that he didn't have any ground. 'Places to put up the tent in the different towns we'll move through,' he expanded when I didn't answer from ten thousand kilometres away.

One time I asked him, 'Why are you never in the pub when I call? Don't you drink?'

'It's safer to drink at home mate, besides, I'm barred from the pub.' Then he laughed deeply. The last phone call came at three in the morning. 'We're going, I've made a deal with my mate Scourge, we can use his ground. I want to leave in five days to make the Maryborough show up in Queensland, and it's a couple of days drive. Can you get here?'

The first thing I noticed about Michael was his smile. It was boundless, unrefined, instinctive. The second was his large forearms. It was only later, racing along the narrow unpaved back roads towards his home in Tullamore, cramped close together in the ute cluttered with tools, chocks of wood, cable, a generator, that I took in the rest. His powerful, unthreatening presence, his long dark plaited pigtail, and the brown, broad, handsome face and black eyes under heavy brows that made you think of a pirate . . . or a warrior.

'I'm a Maori,' and then almost apologetically he told me when I asked. 'We've got to use these back roads, the ute's not road tested,' and then almost apologetically, 'don't want another fine.'

I nodded, gazing through the swirling dust thrown up by a truck that appeared suddenly in front of us, wondering vacantly why the ute was not road tested. 'How far is it?' I asked.

'About 150 kilometres, not far,' he added, unsmiling.

It was turning into evening, the light fading in degrees, softening the bush, making the sheep appear dark and morose. A flock of galahs perched on a dry rotting eucalyptus bough cried frantically as we passed. Later, a small mob of roos moved in a paddock far away, but it was only when they bounded, showing themselves against the greying horizon, that you could distinguish them from the burnt brown grass. Michael chatted, asking questions about my interest in tent boxing, expressing many times his surprise that I wanted to travel with him, wondering about my family, making me feel like we had already known each other for a considerable time.

It was after a lull in our conversation, as we peered through the dust, searching for the road that had temporarily disappeared, that Michael asked, 'You weren't involved in the big brawl the showmen had in Cessnock in the seventies?'

'No,' I answered, 'but I knew blokes who were. But you would have been too young to be a part of that?'

'Yeah,' Michael answered dreamily, 'I was only about ten then, but my brother-in-law told me about it. He said the whole street outside the show grounds was full of brawlers. They were fighting from one end to the other. Rough blokes down your way, he reckons.'

'Yeah, they are, a few mongrels though.' A couple of years after that fight, a group of showies got into a brawl in my pub. They gave the locals a hiding, and then one of the Cessnock boys waited in his car until the showies left the pub, and drove over one of them. Crippling him.

TENT BOXING

TULLAMORE

We arrived in Tullamore, population 400, before dark. Country towns 'far out', can appear almost stealthily. Our ute hit the unannounced strip of dark, even bitumen with little flourish. Signs started to appear, a showground came into view, and a little further, the pub, the one we could never drink in because Michael had knocked out one of its bouncers with a left hook. I heard later that the second bouncer had broke and run.

Around the corner and across the road from the pub was the store that supplied the tools and equipment that were needed to work the land. Their big selling item when I arrived, were troughs used to hand feed sheep. We kept driving straight ahead, past a cafe, a post office, a general store, a newsagency that doubled as a cafe, a hairdresser, and then we were through. At the end of Tullamore's main street, like a sentinel guarding against the towns ruination, stood a solid, towering wheat silo, and across from that, the garage with two petrol pumps that was the only one for thirty kilometres.

Michael's house, an elegant, rambling building built near the edge of the town, was two blocks up from the one-man police station, and one down from the RSL club. Like all Australian houses, it had been constructed to keep out the heat, with no thought being given to the short sharp winters. Inside it was dark and cold.

When we arrived, his five children huddled around us. So, that's how many, I thought. The two youngest girls, Sasha two and Gracie four, falling on Michael, worrying him like hungry puppies, nuzzling him for affection. Michael returned their hugs, behaving like a great bear in spring. His wife Mandy was friendly and hospitable, there was nothing I needed for, nothing she wouldn't do for me. But she was also quiet and still reserved. Perhaps she was withholding judgment, or she still thought I had wasted a trip.

That first evening, Michael and I sat alone on the veranda, resting our backs against the uneven planking, gulping Tooheys Old out of long-neck bottles, wrapped up against the cold wind that blew across the flat empty country.

Earlier, in the hallway of the house, I had noticed photos of grey-haired Maori elders draped in colourful feather cloaks. Their faces, covered in the swirling dark blue tattoos of a warrior, were pinched and unsmiling. I suspected the photos were posed, as if someone needing to document a time already passed had forced the old men to dress up for the camera. When I asked Michael about them, I sensed a stiffness come over him, but there was no moon and the veranda light was ineffectual against the vast blackness, so I could not see his face to confirm it.

I approached the subject carefully, furtively. In Europe, where I had been living almost half my life, races and cultures mixed freely, but the Australia I remembered was suspicious and clannish. 'How does a Maori end up running an Australian boxing tent?'

'My father married the boss's daughter,' Michael answered with no hint of insult. 'I'm born here, so I'm Australian. An Australian Maori,' he added, grinning. I thought then how little I knew about my own country.

'Dad came over in 1958. I think he was about twenty-two then,' Michael began after gulping down the last of his thick dark beer, and placing the empty bottle neatly beside him, lining it up in a row with the other bottles we had emptied that night.

'There was no work in New Zealand in those days, a lot of racism, and I don't think he got on with his father too good. When his brother got a job with Worth's circus that was travelling to Australia, Dad stowed away on the same boat, hoping to get work with them once they arrived. But they caught Dad and put him in jail for a couple of weeks.'

Michael blinked rapidly, unnaturally, before he continued. It was the twitch of a man who had taken a lot of punches to the head. I had seen it before. It was a fighter's affliction.

'By the time they let Dad out, the circus had already left for Western Australia, so he had to take another train over. Three days across the desert in those days.' When Michael paused for the briefest of moments, I turned to stare into the cold wind, towards the moon that had finally appeared, at the light that it threw out, dulling the vivacity of a million stars.

'Dad caught up with the circus in Perth, and they gave him a job. He ended up taking care of the elephants. Old fellas who knew him then, tell me that he was one of the best they ever had.'

'When did he start with Bell's?' I asked, as Michael pushed himself heavily to his feet to fetch more tall black beers. He was half through the doorway before he turned to answer.

'He left the circus in Melbourne, just got tired of it I suppose, might've had some problem. One of old Roy's men saw him walking along, stopped and asked him if he could fight.' When

Michael saw me staring, waiting for an answer, he added incredulously, 'All Maoris can fight.'

I awoke early next morning. When I went into the kitchen to make coffee, I found Michael lying on the lounge, wrapped in a blanket, watching country music videos. The two youngest girls curled under the blanket with him.

He looked at me drowsily. 'I never sleep more than a few hours a night. Mandy doesn't either.'

We drank white coffee together, listening to the sweet strains of Keith Urban singing 'The River' . . . and then I changed into shorts, settled a woollen beanie over my head, and headed out into the cold morning to start a training run that I had been doing for years, aware that I was getting older, fighting it as best I could.

I ran past the outskirts of the town, leaving the last house behind me, following a dirt road that led up a small hill. The road ran past the town dump that swarmed with loud crows, and further into the bush. I stopped when I came to an old heavy ghost gum that reached across the road, shadow sparred in its shadow, careful to dance around a green ants' nest that was also shaded by the tree, and then back. When I returned that first day, I told Michael where I had run.

'It's one of my jobs to keep the garbage tip clean. I've got a little front end loader that I use to push the rubbish in the hole,' he said to me. Then we went to work, preparing for the trip.

Michael planned to use his big white Kenworth to transport equipment and sleep the fighters. It had the odd un-aerodynamic angles and small confined cabin of a truck designed long ago. Its paintwork was dull and blemished, its window scratched and filmy, but its nose was shielded by a bull bar that could protect it from a horse, and its motor was so powerful that it was registered as a road train. Nothing fancy, just watch out.

The trailer had been modified to accommodate travellers. Michael had cut away a section of one side to give better access, covered it with a tight fitting shiny blue tarpaulin that could be folded open and buckled shut on the bottom and side, and installed windows to let in more light. A back section was walled off for storage, and a fibreglass shower cubicle installed. But all this had been done before I arrived.

Our work started by cutting up lengths of steel to make bed frames and welding them to steel spring cots. Ten in total. A boiler was built in, the electric wiring strung, a sink set in place. Toolboxes were welded on, and an old single sleeper cabin, bashed and twisted to fit, was set in place between the cabin and trailer using a forklift. Cut and weld, cut and weld. Michael seemed to have endless work still to do, and I wondered how we were going to be ready in a few days.

Money was always a consideration. Mandy and Michael conferred constantly on ways of saving, on the best way of putting to use the money they had, but I always had a sense that there wouldn't be enough. Michael was a buyer and seller of things, but judging by the trucks, cars and carnival accoutrements littering his back paddock, he was also a hoarder. It was a business filled with inconsistency.

I overheard a deal he was trying to make with an uncle, a Bell on his mother's side. I would catch pieces of a phone call, discussions between husband and wife. Michael wanted to sell a truck and the price was cheap. There was sincere interest, but never an agreement. I had a feeling that the interested party knew Michael's circumstances and was waiting him out. Strange I thought for family, but it was a business deal and people had the right to make the best deal they could. And perhaps I didn't know all the facts.

In the evenings we drank black beers from long-neck bottles, but not before it was dark and never if Michael could still make something ready. It was during one of these drinking sessions that I heard about the farm shed Michael had built for the Dutchman. The biggest one ever erected in the area, the one that had never been paid for, the reason why Michael was so broke and could only sleep a few hours a night.

One afternoon as we sat eating toasted cheese sandwiches and drinking sweet white tea by the fire that had been lit early to chase away the cold, one of Michael's boys arrived home lamenting that he had got into a fight at school with an older, bigger boy. When his mother, who was also drinking tea, asked how it had finished, the boy said that he had told the teacher.

Michael laid both his sandwich and tea mug down and stood, before he told his son with firmness, but without anger, 'It doesn't matter if you lose, son, but never go to a teacher for help. You understand me. It's show-ground law,' he explained to me. 'We never go to the police when we have problems, we handle it ourselves.'

The preparations were dragging on. On the sixth day, we were still cutting and welding the stairs needed to climb up into the trailer; changing motor oil; fitting radios. When I asked Michael about making the Maryborough show, he just shrugged and said we'll aim for Bundaberg a week later.

Locals would drop by, solid men who worked on the surrounding properties. In the ordinariness of their lives, Michael's preparations, his trip, was a colourful distraction, an exotic temptation, but one they would never take up. 'Does he know what he's getting into?' some would ask Michael, as if I were not there and they themselves were experienced tent fighters.

When Michael asked Mandy to drive the 140 kilometres to Forbes to buy the supplies and told me to go along, I knew we were just about ready.

'I want you to talk to my brother Steven. He lives there. He can tell you about Bell's, I forget too much. And I want you to have a look at Dad's grave, Steven will take you.' We took the old black Ford that had belonged to Michael's father Lester. The car that I would be driving on the trip north.

'I'm a show girl,' Mandy told me as we flew along, driving almost as fast as Michael did, fearlessly, skilfully. 'My people and Michael's people are related, but only through marriage. Mum still sells fairy floss and toffee apples at shows.'

I nodded, happy that I was learning something about her. Mandy braked suddenly. I had not been concentrating on the road and braced for a dip, but it was only cattle grazing up ahead.

'Didn't you see the signs?' she asked when she noticed my movements. 'When they warn you like that, you're liable. You have to pay if you hit one of them.'

The cattle were milling peacefully along the sides of the road where the grass grew more thickly. They looked up casually as we passed, but they had seen cars before and soon their heads dropped to continue feeding.

Before speeding up, Mandy reached into her bag and pulled out a packet of Marlboros, shook out a cigarette, deftly clamping it with her mouth and lighting it, ran her hand through her long brown hair, shook it loose, and we raced away. I waited for her to continue the story, but she clutched the wheel tightly, concentrating on the long empty road and said nothing.

A half-hour later, and just before she dropped me off at Steven Karaitiana's house, promising to pick me up later and finish off the shopping, she said very seriously, 'Michael's going to change on this trip. He'll get harder, the showground makes you like that. But don't worry, he'll be all right with you.' I knew then that she had accepted me.

*

Steven drove slowly, reverentially through the well-ordered, sun-bleached cemetery. When we got out and walked the few metres to Rehita Lester Karaitiana's grave, I felt the baked earth crack under my boots.

'Hard isn't it?'

'What?' I asked, not expecting a question, withering in the heat.

'The ground, it's like rock. We were supposed to dig the grave by hand, the Maori way, but in the end we had to give up and bring in a machine to finish it.

I nodded, looking at Lester's headstone, at the inscription 'Forever in the hearts of your loving family' . . . at the gold boxing gloves painted on one side of the headstone, and at the gold guitar on the other, and kicked at the loose gravel that surrounded the grave, not knowing how to answer.

'Michael cut out a couple pieces of the mat that Dad fought on, laid one piece under the coffin, covered it with sawdust, and laid the other piece over the coffin. He must have fought more than four thousand times on that mat. Hundreds came to his funeral.' Steve was a big, powerful man, and it was unsettling to see the emotion stirring in him when he talked about his father, to hear his voice dropping like a weight had been placed on his shoulders, constricting his chest.

'He was a good father?' I asked, for no other reason than to give Steve a chance to calm.

'Aw, look, you couldn't have had a better father. He'd wash, cook, take care of us kids, he wasn't too proud to do anything. He taught us right from wrong.' Steve wiped a trickle of sweat from his forehead with the back of his hand, waited a moment, scuffed the ground, making no impression, and continued, 'Dad put us all through Marist Brothers here in Forbes. It was a private school, Catholics. I still don't know how he could afford that. If the Boxing Tent was close enough, he'd always take us along on our holidays . . . he adored Mum. Let's go!' he suddenly said, and we walked back to the car that had been heated to the temperature of a sauna.

As we drove slowly away, Steve switched on the air conditioner. It roared at first, soaking up the heat, but as the temperature cooled, the roar became a murmur.

'Nice car,' I said.

'Yeah, we're doing all right.'

'What do you do?' I asked, recollecting his imposing house, the new trucks in the yard, the big shed. The order of the place.

'I'm in the show business. I've got a food canteen, rides, a portable stage that I rent out.'

'You work with your family?'

'No,' he answered, 'I did it on my own. I don't have much to do with the Bells.' Steven's phone rang, it was his mother.

I concentrated on the world passing by outside the car window, trying not to listen, but in the confined space it was impossible not to hear words, to feel the warmth. 'She just wanted to know how things were going. Mum calls all the time.'

'How was it when she married your father?'

Steve hesitated, deciding whether it was my business, resolving that it was. 'Her brothers didn't like it too much. I think Uncle Elwin, Mum's twin brother took it the hardest. Colour was a problem in those days . . . all through Australia, New Zealand was no better. When old Roy found out, he kicked them both out.'

'I never knew,' I said. 'Are you angry about that?'

'No,' he answered quickly, 'it was a different time back then, so I can't blame them. Pop was a hard old bugger, but he was a fair man and his word was his honour. Pop and Nana were real good people, just ask any of the fighters that travelled with them. After a couple of years, Dad and Mum came back and worked for Roy.'

'Your dad never held a grudge?'

'Dad was a gentleman, he could never stay angry. Anyway, he always thought of old Roy as his father and in the end he got on all right with his brother-in-laws.'

A car pulled out, cutting us off, bringing a small flush of anger to Steve's face. He relaxed when he saw that it was an old man who had lost the reactions of his youth.

'Still it must have been tough for Dad though because the two brothers were always in charge. It was always family in those days and I suppose Dad was never thought of as real family. They left him to do the hard yakka: taking care of the tent; putting it up and pulling it down, watching over the fighters, do the fighting. Another thing, when Pop died, Dad never got a thing.'

When we got back to Steve's house, his wife served us fried chicken and thickly buttered white bread rolls. 'This is what kills all Maoris in the end; we love our bread and butter,' Steve said, reaching for a roll.

'When did the tent start up again?' I asked, picking at the chicken, refusing the offered bread because I found it a strange combination.

'When old Roy died, the boys didn't want to keep the boxing tent going, so they went into rides and joints. They're the biggest show family in Australia now,' he added as if that were interesting but inconsequential. 'Dad packed up the tent and stored it away. That was around 1970, but the laws were about to change anyway.

'Years later Michael got it out and started up the business again; and don't let anybody tell you that it was one of the Bells who did it.' His voice became louder when he said this, and he tore roughly at a chicken wing, a serious look momentarily flushing away the soft features of his heavy face.

'He did it alone?' I asked, remembering that it had been a family operation, thinking that alone it would have been almost impossible.

'In the beginning Uncle Arnold helped with the spruiking. He was real good, and besides Michael had to do a lot of fighting. Mum handled the money and Dad helped wherever he could. He even had a few fights.'

'What about you, did you give Michael a hand?' I asked, finally accepting a buttered bun, bringing a nod of approval from Steven.

'I had a ride and a couple of games, but I'd fight a lot of the gees. Never liked the real fighting much, I'd leave that to Michael. You know what a "gee" fight is don't you?'

I nodded that I did, chewing slowly, surprised that I enjoyed the taste of the butter, bread and chicken. 'I boxed as a professional, and one time I had to fight a "stew".' The recollection of the fight that wasn't a real fight came back easily because it was my youth, and nobody forgets those days.

'My opponent didn't show, and I had to fight a stablemate. Our trainer told us to go easy, pull our punches, aim to land on gloves. We must have been convincing, because we were thrown a big shower of coins by the public and awarded the best fight of the night.'

Steven smiled brashly but unmaliciously, the way people do who smile often. 'Thought I recognized that nose.'

Then Steve began to describe gee fights, and when he did, his dark eyes danced, his shoulders which resembled bullock hocks lifted unconsciously, protecting his chin. 'It's more like professional wrestling . . . even vaudeville.

'First you got to have a good build up from the spruiker to get the crowd interested. It's just as important as what goes on inside. I'd jump up and down on the board screaming that I would fight anybody, throwing my arms about, making wild Maori battle faces while they pounded the drum harder and harder, and then the bell would join in, and you'd hear a whistle and the drum and bell would stop. The spruiker would start his patter again, and finally one of our fighters who was mingling amongst the crowd would put up his hand. By that time, they'd hate me so much they'd love anybody who had the guts to fight me. And everybody would reckon our bloke was a local.

'When I got him in the tent, I'd spit at him, hit him when he wasn't looking, bite him, kick him, wrestle him to the ground. The crowd would go wild . . . screaming, jumping up and down. The women were just as badly behaved as the men, sometimes worse. If the crowd was right, we'd work it so my mate would win, and as he was walking outside with the mugs, I'd race out and challenge him again. Then we could bring them right back in.'

'Mugs?' I asked.

'A lot of them are, you'll find that out.

'Yeah we'd play plenty of tricks alright,' Steven continued after pausing to reach for more chicken, this time leaving the bread. 'We had an Aboriginal fighter travelling with us called Dennis Cutmore. Dennis could knock out anybody, but he didn't look like much, not big, a bloke you wouldn't normally notice. We would have Dennis standing in the crowd, and when we found a bloke who could fight a bit we would keep bringing him back, letting him win against our fighters. The mugs loved it, and they would keep coming back to see him knock our blokes over. Then we would put him up on the board, and that's when Dennis would put up his hand. Dennis was one of the best tent fighters I ever saw.'

'He's coming with us,' I said, bringing a nod of approval from Steven. 'He'll be our camp boss.'

As I stood to leave, Steven leaned sideways, picked up a guitar that had been resting against his stool and started strumming 'Pearly Shells'. 'It was Dad's favourite,' he said as I walked towards the door where Mandy waited, Sasha perched sideways on her hip. 'He'd play it all the time.'

'Funny, that was a favourite of my mum's as well,' I answered, turning one last time, watching him gently holding the guitar like an oversized baby, thinking I'd never met a Maori who didn't own a guitar, and then trying to remember whether I'd seen one in Michael's house.

'You gunna fight?' he called as I stepped through the door into the outside glare.

'No, too old, I'm finished.' Even from a distance, looking back into the house's soft dark light, I could see his big grin.

When Mandy picked me up from Steve's, she had done most of the shopping. Tin plates, cutlery, cups, buckets, mops, a coffee maker, bread toaster, and great mounds of food lay scattered across the back seat. We drove around looking for a Salvation Army outlet, hoping to buy second-hand blankets, pillows and sheets. In the end, we settled for new bedding at a discount store.

Mandy was moving like someone carrying a great load. There was a lot to do of course, and there was the child to take care of, but I knew her weariness was chronic. Over the previous eight days, I had overheard her doing banking, ordering equipment, organizing the truck and car insurances, and attempting to hunt down fighters who belonged to clannish, suspicious families and whose names or nicknames were given second-hand to Michael during vague telephone conversations.

In fact any notion of Michael's that couldn't be handled by brawn and technical talent would be passed over to her. And all the while taking care of their five kids and us as if we were also her children. She never complained, just carried on, although one time she did tell me how happy she was that I was there to help Michael with the heavy work. 'Otherwise I would have to,' she said.

And then there was the balancing of the books and the ultimate acceptance that all their extra money had to go towards the tour.

She did this without rancour, but it must have added to the burden. At times I thought that Michael without Mandy would be like a one-armed man. I wished that she could travel with us.

We drove back in darkness, watching for roos that raced out of the bush at our oncoming lights like bulls charging a cape. Mandy sipped slowly on a can of Jim Beam and Coke and smoked. The cold breeze drifting through the window left open to keep the air breathable, beat off, if only temporarily, her torpidity. Sasha slept on the back seat on a bed made from the new blankets.

I opened a long neck, searched again for roos in the darkness, gave up when all I could make out was high clumps of shadows that must have been stands of trees, and asked Mandy would she like to come on the tour with us.

She was adamant: 'No, I've done it for years, I've had it. The Aboriginal missions up on the Cape were the worst.' She stopped then, as if that was all that needed to be said.

'What was so bad about them?' I had to ask before she would continue.

'Well, we'd travel up there with a few other show families. They had rides. We had to time it so we arrived on dole day or there wouldn't be any money to make.'

Mandy sipped again at the Jim Beam, placed the can on the gear consol, took a long deep drag of her cigarette and clutched the wheel tightly. 'They loved the boxing tent, any entertainment really, because there isn't much for people to do up there. I suppose that's why they drink so much.' Mandy drew again on her cigarette, reached sideways for her can of Jim Beam, not wanting to take her eyes off the road.

'We would always get good houses, but it was hard to get out to those places; only dirt roads. One time it rained so much, we had to cut down trees, rip the bark off the branches and lay it in front of the truck tyres to get some traction. And we had to pump the water off the road. It took us ten days to travel one hundred kilometres. We ran out of food. Michael took his dog, and went out and shot a couple of wild pigs. That's how we survived.

'Another time we took a boat over to Groote Eylandt to do a show,' she continued, becoming animated. 'I had Karla and Mikey with me and I was pregnant with Marshall. It was so hot and dusty, and we had to sleep in swags and cook on a camp oven. Michael loved it.' She paused, brought her hand to her mouth to draw again on her cigarette, but it was only a pipe of ash down to the filter.

'He got on so well with those people,' she said, after nervously crushing the remains of the smoke in the overflowing ashtray, 'but they were rough, loud places, and it was hard for me to take care of the kids.

'Did Michael tell you about the bloke who got a bashing in one of the tent fights and came back with a spear? That was on Groote Eylandt.' When she saw me staring, my mouth closed over the bottle, she added, 'He got into the tent all right, but his family grabbed him before he could stab anybody. Took a fair few of them to hold him though.'

'How old were you then?' I asked, knowing she must have been not more than a kid herself.

'Twenty-three,' she answered quickly. 'No, I've had enough for a while, maybe when the kids are older. But I'm happy Michael's taking it out again, I believe in the boxing tent. If we are going to make it, it will be with the tent.'

The same evening, after we had eaten the Chinese takeaway made with Australian vegetables, and while we sat on the veranda sipping the long necks that had become our evening ritual, I said, 'Mandy reckons you two had some pretty tough trips together?'

'She told you about them, did she? Did she tell you about working with her old man?'

I shook my head, looking contentedly into the limitless almost lightless night. After living for so long under the heaving masses of dark, foreboding clouds of northern Europe, the Australian sky never failed to fill me with the pride and conceit of a man with a great treasure.

'When she was sixteen or seventeen,' Michael began, blinking wildly, pulling abstractly at his tail of hair which, although still plaited, was dusty and dishevelled, 'she had to sell watches with her old man up in Kings Cross.'

'Is it still rough up there?' I asked, remembering a time when I paid twenty dollars for a prostitute in Kings Cross who was so adept at her work that she had me in and out in six minutes. My mates had timed it.

'Whores, pimps, drunks, junkies, mugs. It'll always be bad up there. They made good money though, but you have to be hard to work the Cross, and Mandy's father was. You know he used to make his two sons put on boxing matches against each other when he had his mates over. They had to punch the hell out of each other. What do you reckon about that?'

'How did you get on with him?' I asked, not bothering to answer.

'We had our moments, but we're all right now. Tell them boys it's getting late!' Michael suddenly called to Mandy when noise of yelling reached us. When he got no reply, 'Boys, get to bed and stop arguing.

'They're always fighting, those two,' Michael said to me with exasperation. 'I'm going to take Mikey with us, separate him and Marshall for a few months, give their mother a break. Anyway Mikey can earn some good money fighting and he's got to get some experience on the show grounds, he's got to take over the tent one day. Next year I'll take Marshall with me.'

Mikey was twelve, but slightly built and with the fine-boned face of an angel. You had to look very closely to see his father's and grandfather's blood. It was the same with all Michael's children. I couldn't imagine Mikey fighting in the tent.

'How was it with Steve?' Michael suddenly asked.

'He told me a bit about Dennis Cutmore. '

'Yeah, Dennis and him put on some terrific gees. You'll like Dennis. I'm happy he's coming, he'll keep the boys in line.'

I nodded and lifted the bottle to my mouth, not thinking about Dennis. 'You two seem a bit different though,' I said, spilling beer accidentally across my chest.

'Yeah, Steve's organized, doesn't have all these old trucks and cars lying about the yard. Some say he's the best equipped to deal with life, but I reckon we've just got different ideas about how to live. We're not getting on too good at the moment.' Michael said this with no bitterness or anger, as if it were just the way it was. But I already knew, because Steven had also mentioned it.

'Did he show you Dad's grave?' Michael nodded contentedly when I answered, and then he drank from the long neck, taking great swallows, not looking at me.

The next day I ran as usual, noticing as I passed the dump that the piles of garbage were growing, that the crows were thicker, their noise more harrowing. I mentioned it to Michael when I got back. He just nodded.

Our first work of the day was to position the double bunks in the trailer. When this was done, Karla was told to make them up with blankets and sheets. We lifted in a small fridge and a large fake leather lounge, and then drove the semi to Michael's workshop. As we drove away from the house, I noticed Mandy carrying clothes draped over one arm towards the small odd-shaped aluminium caravan that would be Michael's and Mikey's home for the next three months.

Lair shirts with embroidery, pearl buttons and colours so bright and brilliant that you could see them for miles. But that was the idea. Black pants, cowboy boots with intricate hand stitching, a bull rider's hat.

In the workshop we loaded the tent pegs and poles, gas bottles, a portable stove, a large red bass drum, a brass bell. It took both Michael and myself to lift the steel box filled with old faded gowns and trunks in a medley of colours into the back of the truck, and again both of us to lift another filled with worn gloves, headgear, boots and bandages.

The steel pipes that slotted into one another and formed the framework for the line-up board were then slid into the trailer along with the boards that the tent boxers would stand on to tempt the locals to fight.

Then, reverentially, we pushed in the long, white, hard-plastic tube, a foot in diameter, that contained the war-paint yellow banners covered with painted portrayals of iconic Australian boxers in fistic poses. Men who had fought in the tent and who in times past had given locals a chance to become legends in their own town, in front of their mates, and with luck, under the gaze of a girl who may have meant something to them.

Lastly, we carried the tightly wrapped bundle that was the tent to the back of the truck, and then, unable to lift it into the trailer, rolled it up a steel ladder like a beer keg.

I was then ordered to climb to the roof of the Kenworth's trailer, and while Michael lifted a generator, an electric welder and two large fake leather armchairs that belonged to the lounge set with the forklift that he used like another limb, I guided them onto the trailer top and tied them down. When we trussed the two king poles that raised up the centre of the tent to bars welded onto the underside of the truck, we were ready.

That afternoon, I drove with Michael perched on the side of his forklift that he had transformed into a front-end loader by changing its tines to a bucket, towards the dump. First checking that the local copper was out of town, because the machine was not registered for use on the road.

I thought that it would take hours to clear away the garbage, but Michael reefed on levers and pressed down peddles that threw his machine into violent jerking movements, raising thick clouds of stinking dust, sending crows into a hateful, frenzied retreat, pushing the garbage into the deep gullies with no more effort than it takes to sweep out a floor.

That was the way he worked: fast, competent. It was not always tradesman standard, but there was almost nothing he couldn't do. Sometimes I felt bad because I had no head to fix or drive things, and all I could offer him was a working back. But he never complained, not once.

In the late afternoon, before the chill and damp of night, we raced back out to the dump, doused the garbage with kerosene, and threw in a match.

'It's against the law now,' he told me as we quickly jumped back into the ute and fishtailed back onto the road into town. 'The greenies put a stop to it, they reckon it pollutes everything. The council'll thank me though, it's the cheapest way to keep the garbage under control. Big fine if I'm caught though,' he said, grinning.

Making a damper, like barbecuing meat, is a task often left to the men in Australia. Perhaps because strength is necessary to knead the flour, water, baking powder and sugar into an elastic compound. Or because wood has to be collected and a fire built, pampered and nurtured until the coals burn a vivid hell red. Or again because a small hole must be dug (although there are men who simply snuggle the camp oven next to the coals) beside the intense heat of the embers, in which the camp oven containing the damper mixture is settled. But it is more likely, because men are more comfortable with the bush, and damper is bush tucker.

Some men leave the damper to take its natural course, knowing through a lifetime of experience when it will be browned crusty on the outside, and cooked light and fluffy with just the right amount of moisture in the centre. Others feel that adding a few coals to the lid of the camp oven, removing some at just the right time, is like sprinkling in a secret ingredient. It is a task of pride, and men take it very seriously. They confer, they worry, they are consumed.

Michael and his mate Boss stood by the oven, adding coals, brushing them away, packing the sides with dirt, then clearing it away, while Mandy and Allene, Boss's wife, sat away from the fire under the protection of a three-sided tin shed chatting amiably, like good friends do. The younger children played on the bare red earth, running wildly around the water tower, the wood heap, the parked utes and cars, ducking under the fold-up table that held the salads, fruit cakes and half drunk long-neck bottles, squealing delightedly. And when you least expected, the boys would shoot past on their bicycles, one wheel high in the air.

Above and beside the damper, another camp oven full of wild rabbit, potatoes and squash, hung precariously from a tripod of steel bars over the fire. The trees around us glowed golden, as if the setting sun that dropped behind them had jaundiced the bush.

I sat unneeded on a plastic chair, beside the fold-up table, picking absently at a photo that had been left on the table between the salad bowl and the cake tin. It was faded and misty. Men wearing ill-fitting, rumpled pinstripe suits and brimmed hats, stood looking up at fighters standing on the Line-up Board. Behind the fighters hung a banner, but the boxers, who appeared to be mostly Aboriginals, and who all wore heavy boxing gowns, obscured the view, leaving only glimpses of letters. The hint of a likeness.

I recognized Roy Bell, small, jacketless, wiry, wearing a white shirt and a bowler hat, from a photo Michael had shown me of him a few days earlier. He was facing one of his fighters, crouching slightly, the way you do when talking to someone who is important or dangerous. I knew he was introducing one of his fighters to the men below, spruiking him into something larger than life. Someone who would guarantee your immortality, but only if you had the mettle to step into the ring with him. The old photo was taken before the war, during the Great Depression, when men had nothing. The crowd was spellbound. I knew this, because in a different era I had stood in just such a crowd.

When Michael saw me looking at the photo, he walked away from the damper, returned to the fire, brushed a few more coals from the top of the oven with a shovel, and then pulled a chair up beside me.

'Every top fighter in Australia fought for Pop at one time or another: George and Eddie Bracken, little Bindi-Jack, black as coal was Bindi, Dave and Alfie Sands, Jack Hassen, Vic Patrick, Ron Richards, the Alabama Kid, Don Bronco Johnson, even Jimmy Carruthers.'

I knew them all. They had been champions of Australia in the days when boxing had been popular and esteemed. Jimmy Carruthers had gone on to win a world title when he battered the little South African Vic Toweel into submission in just one round, and the great Aboriginal fighter Dave Sands certainly would have won a world title had his own truck not rolled on top of him and crushed him to death only weeks before the fight.

Those boxers came out of an era when men fought with six-ounce gloves, and a title fight went fifteen rounds. When crowds filled boxing stadiums and gave their unyielding support and respect to fighters. And why wouldn't they? It took guts to step into a ring that you couldn't get out of until the fight had gone the long bruising distance, or until you were beaten bloody and beyond obvious redemption, or you quit: but the real ones never quit.

They belonged to a time where opportunity was limited; an uncompromising era, but one where humility and good conduct were commonplace. A better time, or so I had often been told.

'Don Bronco Johnson,' I said, his name jolting my memory, and then the image of swollen disfigured eyebrows, a nose that had grown and twisted with each punch so that it resembled a misformed potato, the thick, scarred hands. 'Rough fighter,' I added.

Michael gave a cheeky grin. 'The roughest, he turned every fight into a war, you had to knock Bronco out or kill him before he would stop. A good bull rider too.'

Boss came over, walking sideways, one eye on us, the other on the damper. He carried a shovel one handed, like a cook with a tasting spoon.

'Michael's grandfather always used to camp around here between the Queensland and NSW runs.'

'That's right,' Michael answered, taking up the story. 'One of his daughters ended up buying a property near here. When she did, Pop always stayed with her. It was their holiday. Pop and Nan are buried in the Tullamore cemetery. This whole area has sort of become part of the Bells' history.'

Michael then walked back to the fire, gently taking the shovel from his friend's protesting hand as he passed.

'Have you always lived up here?' I asked. 'When you're not travelling with the show I mean.'

'No,' Michael answered, playing with the ashes again. 'We were in Sydney for a while, but it's better up here. Can't get into too much trouble. Here it's better for the kids to grow up in too.' I nodded, wondering what trouble he was talking about, but he had already begun to tell another story.

'One time when the troupe was resting up,' he said, staring into the fire, gauging its heat, 'Bronco Johnson bailed up a half wild horse in a paddock, bolted onto his back with a .303 and shot two roos at full gallop. He had to go to Sydney for a while and he wanted to leave his missus with some tucker.' Michael was shaking his head in astonishment when he added, 'Steered the mad bastard through the scrub with the barrel of his rifle, just touching the horse's head when he needed to turn him.'

'She was an Aboriginal?' I asked, just as astonished.

Michael waited for another spasm of blinking to pass, 'Always had Aboriginal women. I reckon he must have thought they were easier to take care of. Anyway, they were probably the only women tough enough to live with him. My aunt's husband took her down some food when he found out. Can't leave somebody with just a couple of roos to eat.'

They both cleared the oven of its last coals. 'It's ready,' Michael's mate called in a loud even voice filled with pride.

When they turned the camp oven upside down, the damper fell solidly, loudly onto the table. I was offered the crust. 'The best part,' I was told. I buttered it gingerly, trying not to break it, dunking it into the rabbit stew that I had ladled onto a plate, hoping to soften it. It had been burned coal black and tasted like brittle charcoal.

'Beautiful,' was the verdict of the men. I waited for the old dog to wander by before I let it discreetly fall, took a long swig from the long neck, and sucked on a piece of the sweet, stewed rabbit.

The following morning, I felt an acrid itch deep in my chest as I jogged up the hill towards the dump, and when I reached the rise I came face to face with plumes of thick cold-dust black smoke rising above and drifting menacingly away from the garbage dump. Holding low; tree height to ground. The crows were perched upwind, discontented and quarrelsome, like old maids forced to live together in a barren, prudish life. I turned and headed back to town, unwilling to risk the sprint I would have to make through poison to continue my training.

When I got back, I found Michael sitting at the kitchen counter, drinking coffee, both hands around the mug, almost concealing it, blinking, staring, pensive.

'How's the fire?' he finally asked, and when I told him it was still burning, he said it would take a while. Then we began loading the food, leaving the meat, just some fat pork sausage and bacon, till last.

'I don't want those fighters causing any trouble on the show grounds,' Michael said, while carrying a bag of potatoes hoisted over one shoulder, and a box filled with tin, stewed meats, powdered milk and sugar snuggled under the other arm. 'I'm going to tell them there's going to be no visitors and no drinking in our camp. Dennis'll keep them in line.' He said this out loud, but he was speaking to himself as well as to me. 'Don't get involved in anything, Wayne. You hear an argument or a fight going on, ignore it.'

I knew the showmen would be hard, but Michael was hinting at something more menacing. I nodded, wondering how bad it could be.

Michael still had no fighters. He had been trying to get some white heavyweights from Sydney, and a local professional from Dubbo, but nobody had committed. Michael had also heard about two Aboriginal fighters from Gunnedah who might be interested.

The white fighters declined, and the Aboriginals from Gunnedah were not to be traced. Uncles and grandmothers of the Aboriginal fighters had been reached, but Mandy couldn't allay their suspicion that we meant them harm in some way.

'We'll get enough fighters in Moree,' Michael told me when I expressed my anxiety that you can't have a travelling boxing troupe without boxers. 'It's the toughest town in Australia, it's Dennis's town. He's already got six blokes lined up.'

I knew Moree was a tough place. Thirty years before, I had worked as a bank teller in Mungindi, a baking bush town straddling the NSW – Queensland border, that was located only 140 kilometres north of Moree.

In Mungindi, we were shielded from its infamy by deep-rutted gravel roads, and a reputation as a quiet backwater, but we heard the stories of race violence, we knew about the bitter pub battles between white and black, the past segregation in the picture theatres, and the outright ban on Aboriginals in the city swimming pool, the brutality of the police.

I played league with the local team, 'the Mungindi Grasshoppers'. A mission of scorching tin and timber houses built on a treeless flat on the edge of town housed our Aboriginal population. The Mungindi team was for the greater part Kamilaroi Aboriginals, the same mob as Moree. But we never had the trouble they had. Granted, Mungindi was a segregated community, and colour prejudice existed, but at times we drank together, and when we played rugby league, it was as a team.

One sweltering Saturday I stood by the bar of a low-built timber pub, just across the bridge on the Queensland side. The pub was shaded by thickly leaved gum boughs that stretched across its tin roof like the arms of a doting mother. I drank with our fullback, a fast wiry man with a shallow work scar running out from the corner of his lip to his cheek. He wore a holed, sweat-stained grey Akubra hat, and riding boots because he was a working man. He paid his drinks like all working men do.

It was during the euphoria of our drunkenness, at a moment of camaraderie that can never be matched under sober circumstances. Before he drove me out to the mission to meet his sister who was taller than him, and whose almond eyes were much deeper and larger, and who stood on the small porch of their mission home, barefoot, in a faded floral dress. Before she told me that she would rather go out with a lizard than with me, that my mate mentioned he didn't like going into Moree. 'Nobody does from around here, there is always trouble.' Mungindi was a better town.

Years later, I would learn about protest actions that had taken place in Moree. Marches, riots. The time Charlie Perkins, a black activist rented buses and filled them with Aboriginal kids, drove to the city swimming pool, and encouraged them to throw eggs in the water before storming its gates.

'Hotel Bomb Blast', 'Court told of threat to blow up the town.' Two Aboriginal men, one a powder monkey and the other a young labourer, had used twenty sticks of gelignite to blow up the Imperial Hotel in Moree in 1976.

I remembered it clearly, because it had only happened a short while after I had left Mungindi, and because people didn't blow things up in Australia.

A few details lodged solidly in my mind: they blew the pub up because, as Aboriginals, they were refused service. 'It was a political statement,' one of them had said, and that the younger of the bombers had cried when talking to the police. He had done so when he saw the wreckage of the hotel, and because he had thought for a moment that people must have been hurt or killed. Miraculously, although the hotel was full of guests and staff, no one was. Yes, I knew Moree was a tough place.

Michael spray painted the undercarriage of his truck, because he wanted it to look as good as it could when we drove onto the show grounds, past his mob . . . the showmen. He did it quickly, roughly,

28

because we had run out of time. Then, using the forklift to lift them into position, he chained on the spare truck tyres to the front of the trailer, hooked the old silver caravan onto the black 88 Ford with the big six motor, and we said our goodbyes.

There were tears from the youngest girls, but the Karaitianas were a show family who had said goodbye often, and they did so with little fuss. Mikey looked small and apprehensive sitting on the front seat of the Kenworth next to his dad, who was all smiles and great heaving waves as he battled to get the truck swung around and onto the road leading out of town.

I waited until the truck pulled away, until it sounded its horn like a charging bull elephant, fumbled with the automatic shift that had lost its gear indication cover, and pulled jerkily out, following uneasily. We were out of town and off the bitumen in minutes.

Michael pulled the truck over a few miles further on. We all got out and walked to the Tullamore graveyard. Michael's grandparents were buried side by side. Next to his grandfather's grave was another. Its headstone read: 'In memory of a dear friend, Johannes Tops, born Estonia 1897, died . . .' The rest was not to be deciphered.

'He was a wrestler,' Michael said, looking down at the grave of his grandfather, answering my question distractedly. 'He was with Pop for years. Even during the war when the tent wasn't working. They made charcoal together. Pop said he was one of the strongest men who ever lived. My dad wanted to be buried next to Pop too,' Michael added, before mumbling something that I couldn't hear.

Michael was already in his truck cabin writing in his trucking logbook when I asked him what he had said. 'I was asking Pop to travel with us,' he said, seriously . . . unembarrassed.

ON THE ROAD

I followed nervously in the thick blinding dust thrown up by the Kenworth, until Michael's voice came on the two-way radio telling me to drop back. I did, lighting a cigar, learning by and by to control the pull of the van on the gravel, enjoying the softness a weakened afternoon light can give a hard, burnt country. Distracted momentarily by grazing sheep; a machine throwing dust up in a faraway paddock; a lone tree, seeming to carry the weight of all the felled trees meant to be shading a sensitive, vulnerable land. Hitting the bitumen just on dark.

We drove north through Coonabarabran, and on towards Narrabri; a trucking route. Wide open spaces, but the wind had picked up and the clouds, which were dense and dark, raced across the night, curtaining the moon, letting sparing shards of light escape, allowing only glimpses of silhouettes. But the road trains gave me little time to look.

When I glanced in the side mirrors, I would see lights . . . miles back I thought, but then they were on me, metres away from the back of the caravan, chasing like sniffing dogs on a worn-out bitch; frustrated and angry that they couldn't pass easily. And when they did, it was always with recklessness, and more than once I had to pull off the road to let them back in.

There were times when I grew used to them and disregarded their honking, ignored their flashing lights, even tried to show them courtesy, because I was so much slower, but always their dangerous urgency would start me yelling, although they couldn't hear me, or showing them the finger that they wouldn't have time to notice, or smashing my fist against my own window in anger, wanting to fight them all.

I pulled into the truck stop on the outskirts of Narrabri, seven hours after I'd left Tullamore, an hour before midnight, relieved that I had made it, and more confident that I could handle the long roads ahead. Michael had his Kenworth parked, and was waiting patiently for the arrival of his caravan . . . his bed.

We ate hamburgers and drank coffee in the near empty garage restaurant, served by a weary, motherly, middle-aged woman, who fussed over Mikey like he was an orphaned angel, and then we slept. Next morning before daylight we drank more coffee served by the same waitress, and then we were gone, heading for Moree.

Light comes fast on the plains. After the morning sun lifts above the Pacific Ocean in the east and climbs over the Great Dividing Range, the country changes quickly from muted shades to blinding vividness. And because we were heading north, and there were no clouds to dull it, the sun bounced off my windscreen like someone reflecting light from a mirror. Fortunately the roads between Narrabri and Moree are straight, and if you squint with one eye, lowering your gaze to concentrate on the immediate road ahead, you can keep a focus until the sun rises higher and ceases to be a bother.

Tuffie's apartment in Moree was small, ordered and homely. He welcomed Michael like a long lost son, first serving us tea, and then checking that Mikey was not hungry. When Mikey said he wasn't, he made meat sandwiches anyway.

31

He was still stringy and agile at fifty-eight, still had the pointy, boyish face he had when he was a young Roy Bell's tent fighter. He still moved briskly, seeming not to be bothered by his middle-aged paunch, but the smokes had ruined his breathing.

They called him Tuffie, not because he had been a long-serving, hard-as-nails ring man, but because he had been the only kid in his mob not to have succumbed to a childhood disease that killed a lot of his mates. Tuffie made a phone call and a few minutes later, Dennis Cutmore walked in.

When the three of them huddled together to discuss the trip, it was like watching a meeting of clan elders. Dennis had bad news, most of the men who said they would come, had backed out.

We unhooked the caravan, piled into the black Ford and started our search around Moree for anybody who had showed interest. Michael thought he could talk them around.

We left Tuffie's neat apartment block built on manicured lawn, and drove through streets of council housing projects, passing empty, overgrown lots strewn with broken bottles and rusting cans. Passed pubs where the boys like to drink, idled in front of houses where they might be living, only to be told that nobody knew where to find them. We came across a sixteen-year-old Aboriginal boy with Chinese eyes who still wanted to come, but his father said no.

Finally, we drove to the mission section, an area near the river where all Moree Aboriginals had been forced to live at one time, and pulled up in front of a house that was falling apart. The front door was hanging and the front windows were broken. There was an old rusting car in the yard. Before Michael could turn off the engine, Mauler and Leroy appeared at the front door.

'You coming, Mauler?' Dennis yelled through the open car window, not bothering to get out of the car.

They had been drinking, but their walk through the long, pale grass was steady. Mauler, whose head was large and Slavic looking, was much the heavier and taller of the two. Leroy, who stumbled as he neared us, was darker and ten years older. When he reached the car, he spat heavily, bringing up bile along with the spit, and then cleared his nose on the grass, closing one nostril with a finger. The grog had sickened him.

'Yeah, I'm coming, let me get a bag.' When he said this, I could feel Michael change, a tension that was hard to spot unless you knew him a bit disappeared. He had his Take.

I'd overheard Michael, Tuffie and Dennis mention Mauler many times. He was the one who really counted. When I asked them what a Take was, they told me it was a man who could fight anybody and win.

'Leroy, you want to come?'

'I'm no tent fighter.'

'You can hit, Leroy, I've seen ya.' But Leroy was spitting again, not listening.

'Can he hit?' Michael asked Dennis, leaning towards him so Leroy couldn't hear.

'Yeah, one time I seen him knock a bloke out at the pub. I know he did some boxing years ago too.'

'Come on, Leroy, it's easy, only three one-minute rounds, big gloves. I'll look after you, no hard fights, and I pay cash. You got family here?' Michael asked, thinking that might be the reason he didn't want to come.

'No, I got a missus and three kids, but they're in Coffs Harbour.'

Michael nodded. 'You can earn some good money with us.'

Mauler then took Leroy aside and almost in a whisper said, 'Leroy, we can still pick up our dole.'

'But I don't want to let you down, Michael. I might not like it, Michael,' Leroy answered, turning away from Mauler as if he had not heard him.

'You don't like it, Leroy, I'll put you on a bus back.'

'All right, I'll give it a go, Michael.' But he wasn't looking at Michael and his voice was breaking when he said it. I couldn't tell whether that was because he was still unsure, or because he was fighting off fits of nausea or holding back spurts of coughing. He walked back into the house and returned in moments with a bag.

Leroy and Mauler sat in the back seat with me. Leroy lit up a smoke, still mumbling that he hoped he wouldn't let Michael down. As we drove away, he turned to me to ask how it worked but was overtaken by a coughing fit that forced him to lean out of the window to dry retch. Mauler, who was also smoking, told him he shouldn't think about the fighting, only about the women they would get, because women loved fighters.

'Michael,' Mauler suddenly said, as if the thought had just come into his head, 'my house is about to fall down. They're gunna give me another one, but I got to pay a couple of month's rent, and I can't leave before I pay it because they want to kick me out.'

Michael looked at Dennis for confirmation, and when he nodded his head, Michael said, 'All right, Mauler,' and we drove straight to a small, inconspicuous office run by an Aboriginal organization, where Michael paid the money.

We drove back to Tuffie's to pick up Mikey, hitched the caravan back on to the Ford, and an hour before dark, headed north. Dennis rode with Michael in the Kenworth, Mauler moved in beside me on the front seat. Leroy settled on the back.

We drove north towards Boggabilla, which was just due east of Mungindi, across flat, sizzling country on a sealed, usable road. When I worked at Mungindi all those years ago, the roads in all directions were corrugated gravel. They could shake the life out of anything, or twist and tip you at the slightest loss of concentration. But in those days, we drank a lot, and that was the most likely reason why the roads were so unforgiving. Michael told me that when his grandfather started out, there were only forty-five miles of sealed road in all of Australia, and almost no bridges.

Mauler stretched out as much as his big frame allowed, removed his boots and smoked, studying the passing bush like a cartographer drawing maps, squeezing at his jaw that I noticed was deeply and widely scarred down one side.

'How did you get the scar?' I asked.

'My ex-missus hit me with a brick.'

He then showed me a deep indentation on his thigh where the same woman had stabbed him. When I asked him why, he just said, 'We was drunk and fight'n,' as if that was all the excuse needed to attempt murder.

I lit a cigar awkwardly, pondering this domestic violence, filling the car temporarily with pungent blue smoke that I preferred to the bitter ash grey of Mauler's cigarette, and then glanced into the rear-view mirror to check on Leroy. I found him curled up like a nursing baby, arms wrapped together, snorting fitfully.

I pulled in behind the big Kenworth when we reached the little border town. It was almost dark. Michael had parked across from a pub called The Wobbly Boot Hotel. He walked stiffly to our car, stretching out his arms, loosening the sockets, twisting and rolling his big neck.

'There's a mission near here, Mauler. Do you know anybody?'

'They're the same mob as us. Probably get some fighters. It's out of town a few miles though.'

Michael thought a moment. 'Go and have a look in the pub, you might find somebody. We don't have time to go running out to the mission, I want to keep going.'

Mauler jumped out. 'Leroy, get up, we going to the pub. Michael, you got some money, we need smokes?' Michael gave them enough to get a couple of beers as well. 'I'll put it on the books,' he said. And they were gone.

Dennis had a ponderous, menacing walk. His long arms hung straight down from big round shoulders, but he spoke with a quiet voice, and more often than not he dropped his head, not looking at you when he talked. It was hard to imagine that he had bashed hundreds of men into unconsciousness.

'I'll ride with the boys, Michael.'

'You want to drive?' I asked, understanding that Dennis was the camp boss, my boss. He dropped his head and said, 'No, you drive if you don't mind, I don't see too good in the dark.' Fighter's eyes, I thought.

'What's your name anyway, Little Fella?'

I told him my name was Wayne, but from then on he only ever called me Little Fella.

Mauler and Leroy returned carrying long necks, and leading a stocky, unshaven man. 'This is Jonno, his family are Richards, same as the Richards mob down our way.'

'Is he coming?' Michael asked, unconcerned about any family affiliation.

'No, he wants to come, but he can't because somebody died on the mission and nobody can leave for a week. It's our law.'

Jonno had red drunk's eyes and a swagger, and when he saw me he glared. Perhaps he was only trying to focus, or he was concentrating the way you need to when you've temporarily poisoned your brain, trying to figure out what I was doing amongst his mob. We drove off as Jonno headed back to the pub, swaying, not looking back.

Dennis took the front seat. We had been travelling north for over 600 kilometres, and the weather was warming, but as night came it cooled quickly and a breeze picked up. When Mauler and Leroy started complaining about the temperature, I wound up the window and we continued driving in a cloud of cigarette smoke.

Traffic was rare, but each time a truck passed us on the narrow roads, I was blinded and forced to blink madly, fighting the glare and my own bad eyes as powerful lights shone through the scratched, filmy window. Crossing the crest of a hill and coming face to face with a road train was like being isolated and illuminated under a spotlight.

Dennis and the boys talked unceasingly about Moree. It was macabre gossip, but told in normal tones, with no obvious exaggerations or excitement, and completely impartial.

They spoke about bashings, kickings and stabbings within families, about people who had been jailed and for how long, and why. I heard Mauler complaining that there were a lot more stand-over men in Tamworth prison than in any other he'd been in, and then he added that the biggest tribal group in Tamworth jail was the Moree mob. When I glanced in the rear-view mirror, I saw Leroy nodding his head in agreement. Dennis talked about his own son being in prison, but then he used a different voice, lower, sadder.

'Michael told me that you did some fighting, Little Fella.'

'Yeah, mostly down in Sydney,' I answered, thinking that Dennis wanted to change the subject. 'I had a few fights up in Newcastle . . . trained with Ron Short.'

I glanced sideways at Dennis when I said this, giving my eyes a momentary rest from the road. He had a heavy, amiable, light-coloured face. His brown hair was longish, and seemed like it should have belonged to a younger man. Jealously I ran my hand over my own, which was cut close and thinning.

Later when I studied his face again, I realized how much lighter it was than Mauler's. You would hardly know Dennis was Aboriginal, I thought.

'Wog.'

'What, Mauler?'

'You want a drink?'

'No,' Dennis answered.

'They call you Wog?' I asked.

'Yeah, that's what they call me in Moree. They reckon I look like an Italian.'

'You've got Italian blood?' I asked, surprised.

'My father's a German. When he was young, he had blonder hair than yours, and green eyes. He was real tall.'

'And your mother?' I asked.

'She's a Moree woman.'

'Have you always lived around Moree, Dennis?'

'Yeah. We lived in a tin humpy down by the river until I was a teenager. Happy times, Little Fella. Lots of aunts, uncles and cousins to play with.' He paused thoughtfully before he said, 'You don't need much to make you happy when you're a kid.'

'What happened to your father?'

'Mom threw him out when we was kids. We might see him though, he lives in Rockhampton. He's been trying to get in touch with me. I'm not sure yet. I might see him. Supposed to be a rich man.'

Mauler and Leroy dozed, Dennis seemed content to watch the road ahead, glancing now and then at the bush that was only different shades of blackness.

'I fought one of Ron Short's boys in Newcastle once. He was a little blond fella like you. I knocked him out.' Dennis said this still looking at the road ahead.

We drove north up to Moonie, which is only a crossroads on flat grain country, filling up with coffee, sandwiches and petrol, before turning towards the north-east and heading through Dalby and then Kingaroy, aiming for Bundaberg on the coast. Just before midnight, we pulled to the edge of the road to sleep. Each time a truck passed, the trailer rocked gently as if it were a boat being lifted by small waves. Michael made me park the caravan in front of the Kenworth as a precaution against a driver who might pull sleepily off the road . . . on top of us.

Early the following morning, we drove away from the red dirt country, through the town of Murgon and stopped. We cooked up a feed of canned beef stew on a small gas stove, mopping our plates with white bread and butter, using the Ford's bonnet as our breakfast table. While we were heating water for coffee, Michael told me that he wanted me to go back to Cherbourg to look for fighters.

When Michael, Mikey and Dennis pulled out onto the highway, heading down towards the coast in the Kenworth, I checked that the caravan was securely fastened to the old black Ford, that the brake lights were hooked up, and then I turned the Ford around, heading back the way I'd come.

Cherbourg mission was established when people from the Waka Waka tribe settled in the hilly, pine and eucalyptus country just outside of Murgon in 1904. In 1986 it was authorized to run its own affairs by the state and federal government, and the Cherbourg community council was created. Cherbourg is an Aboriginal town, the oldest and largest self-governing community in Australia.

'They's all Murris here, Leroy.'

Leroy, who lay flat on the back seat, still ill from his Moree drinking binge, raised himself and looked about. Disinterestedly at first, but then Mauler's enthusiasm became infectious, and both became excited by the houses that were sturdy and cared for, the big working timber mill on the hill, the main street with its shops and community centre, the parks that were being cleaned as we passed, and by their own people.

'Shit, in Moree the parks are full of empty beer bottles and drunks,' Mauler said with amusement, but also, I suspected, with astonishment.

I pulled the old caravan around the town and then around again. People began to notice us. The police drove by, and then they drove by again. We were searching for a Moree man who had married into the community, because Mauler thought he could help us find fighters, but Mauler seemed reluctant to ask his whereabouts. These people were a different mob, maybe that was it, or maybe Mauler was just shy. Sometimes he would yell out, 'Hey brother/Hey sister, do you know Jack Kelly?' But nobody knew.

I pulled up in front of a group of men and boys standing on a corner. They were people who had nothing to do. Every town has them.

'Do you know any boxers?' I asked them, because Mauler and Leroy wouldn't. They sent me up a street to a green house. A boy came out to talk to us – a seventeen-year-old welterweight.

He would like to come he said, shuffling shyly in his doorway, but he had to pick up a school award in Brisbane the following week. We talked to him and told him how easy it would be, and how much money he would earn and made promises that we would put him on a bus to Brisbane in five days. When his mate, who was also a boxer, turned up and said that he would like to come, I knew we had them. Zac and Chris, the Cherbourg boys, just right for the young fellows who would want to have a go. I expected there would be plenty.

First we needed permission from Zac's mother. There was no mention of a father, nor of Chris needing any sort of consent. We drove to the high school that was large and modern, and one that we had already noticed while driving around Cherbourg looking for Jack Kelly. The mother, who was a teacher at the school, was suspicious and reluctant, but when Zac told her how much he wanted to travel with us, she agreed. We exchanged phone numbers and I promised again that we would have them on a bus in five days.

She sent him off with no outward signs of affection, only inquiring whether he had enough clean clothes, and warning him not to get to Brisbane late. We piled into the Ford, and rolled down the hill heading out of Cherbourg, towing the high-riding silver caravan like an extravagant bustle.

'Hey, do you boys know where we can get some yanni?' Mauler asked.

They did, because they were tough boys and knew what was going on and where, but they were adamant that they didn't drink or smoke themselves. I told Leroy and Mauler that they would have to wait until Bundaberg to buy dope.

'We need to get going,' I said, which was the truth, but I also wanted to keep drugs out of the car. It had been a long time since I had travelled in Queensland, but the last time I had, *Playboy* was thought too provocative to be sold publicly, and the Queensland police had a grim reputation, especially when it came to dealing with pot smokers and Aboriginals. Maybe things had changed, but I hadn't heard.

I also felt a responsibility to the Cherbourg boys and to Zac's mother to keep them out of trouble. That's what I told myself anyway, but maybe it was just that Europe, my home for the last eighteen years, with its oppression of laws and regulations had taken any of the Ned Kelly out of me.

Leroy began to protest, but when Mauler told him that they would get plenty of yanni in Bundaberg, they both lit cigarettes, settled back to take a last look at the community that is responsible for its own existence, filling the car with smoke, forcing Zac and Chris to lean towards the open window, searching for breathable air.

We crossed the range that separates the hinterland from the coast in the early afternoon, and rode down into Bundaberg off a breaking wave of sugar cane. Houses raised on stilts and imprisoned by the high sweet crop appeared intermittently like besieged grasshoppers amongst a swarm of ants.

'Hey, where's the show ground, bro?' Mauler yelled to a man standing in front of a house. He never said excuse me, please or thank you. Dennis had pointed this out.

BUNDABERG

We saw the Ferris wheel first; still kilometres away. The gondolas, sheltered with plastics roofs of primary colours, orbited unhurried and deliberate, like an overseer supervising a great magical construction. Horse trailers and cattle trucks blocked our path as we neared the gate. Inside, it was a chaos of trucks and trailers, half-built rides, joints and food canteens. A great caterwauling of noise and colours.

Laughing, scowling, muscular men shrouded with tattoos and smeared in grease, bolted together vibrantly coloured machines meant to catapult you into the sky at great speed, or drop you until your guts filled your throats, or allow you to fly like a bird, or revolve as if you were an egg in a beater.

Some were constructing gentler, slower rides meant for children: gaily painted teacups that spun slowly around, while orbiting a jewel-studded teapot; boats fashioned as ducklings floating on a plastic pond; slow comical trains that held to their hilly winding tracks like snails sliding across a brick wall.

Laughing clown heads lay about like sinister miscreations, boxes of pink, green, yellow and purple soft toys were piled in the sun, waiting the construction of their joint, where they would be offered up as prizes to winners at the shooting gallery, the hoop-la booth, the lucky envelope, bust the balloon and can joints.

We drove further into the body of the grounds, winding through sideshow alley, past show-bag concessions, food canteens, the Great Mousco Circus, where mice rode on miniature swings, turned over and around on contraptions that resembled the Ferris wheel, ran willy-nilly through wire tunnels and up wire steps: past the half-built haunted mansion with its facade of fiends and monsters, coming at last to an empty space across from the exhibition hall housing exceptional chickens, near another with caged, exotic birds.

Dust raised by the movement of vehicles and construction was thick, and in the dry windless air, it lingered, finally settling, covering everything.

There was little fuss when we arrived. The boys were introduced and Michael put us to work unloading the Kenworth while he drove the caravan to another area set aside for living.

We built up the camp first, stretching out a tarpaulin from one side of the Kenworth, and raising it with poles. Set up a plank table and chairs under the tarpaulin, brought out the gas stove, food boxes, the plates and cutlery, buckets and basins to wash up in.

When Michael returned, he showed us how to connect up the hoses for water, and where to run the lines for electricity. Leroy shimmied up to the roof of the Kenworth and lowered down the lounge chairs that were placed in the shade next to the Kenworth. Lastly, we hauled an old blue boxing bag from the back of the Kenworth, lifted it to the roof of the truck, and then dangled it by a rope from a bent metal pipe that slotted into a corner of the trailer frame.

Showmen wandered by wanting to talk to Michael because he was one of them, and he was back. All of them acknowledged

Dennis, giving him their hand, remembering his fights, discussing them with admiration.

'You see, Little Fella, they all know me. Did you know I once had twenty-four fights in one day? People don't forget things like that. Sometimes I even got drunk before fighting, just to give my opponents a chance.' Dennis said that with his hands in his pockets, his shoulders turned in, his hair falling across his face. He said it almost bashfully.

The boys had not yet been paid, and their smokes were finished. Anybody who came near Mauler suffered under the same demand, 'Hey, got a smoke?' Leroy was more polite. 'Can you spare a smoke, bro?' Dennis and I watched in amusement as men and boys gave cigarettes freely, never quite game enough to say no. But they only ever bludged from the show staff, never from the showmen. They had already learnt their place in the social order that Michael had hinted at in Tullamore.

We drank coffee and then began to unload the trailer. It was hot and we moved slowly, fatigued from three days on the road, quick meals, long distances. Michael set us into teams. Under his supervision, Mauler and Leroy assembled the frame for the line-up board. Pipes fitting into pipes, setting the heavy entrance gates in place, and hanging the bright yellow banners announcing Bell's Touring Stadium of Boxers and Wrestlers. 'Stake them down with the steel pegs,' he ordered.

The rest of us pulled the tent out of the trailer, unfolded it, laying it in position behind the line-up board, and began driving in the pegs that held it in place. Learning to swing the heavy hammers, to double hit; one man and then the next.

The ground was hard and we tired quickly, but there were five of us and Michael was worth two. When the pegs were in, we lifted the tent in the corners and along the sides with poles, tied them off to the steel pegs and ran in the king poles. When the two king poles were raised, the blue and red tent lifted like a party dress billowing in a wind. While Michael hung the lights and speakers, and connected them to the electrics, the rest of us assembled the side walls.

'Mauler, hang up the flags!' The Union Jack and Southern Cross on a night blue background. And then there was only the five-metre-square piece of canvas boxing mat to peg out.

'We'll do it later, we don't fight until tomorrow night,' Michael said as he walked away with a small man with a broken front tooth and long straggly hair. He had already introduced me to Scourge who had a warm ingratiating smile, a swollen right hand and a big square gold ring that could be mistaken for an expensive knuckle-duster.

Michael turned back and said, 'Wayne, take Dennis and Mikey and go and buy some food. We'll have a drink later. I got to talk to Scourge about business.'

I nodded, and then turned to Mikey who was talking to another boy about the same age. 'Bring your mate if you want.'

Mikey loved to shop, and gave me one of his big smiles. The other boy scowled at me the way the rich look at beggars and walked away.

'What was that all about?' I asked Dennis, who had been standing near me.

Dennis chuckled. 'Some of them showmen teach their kids young that they're the boss, and the staff is not worth much.'

'He's eleven years old,' I said astonished, 'and this is Australia. It's like a fucking Hindu caste system.'

'Well, I don't know what you mean by a caste system, but that's the way it is on the showgrounds.'

We came back with the basics: chops, sausages, potatoes, eggs, bread, onions, a cabbage, a cauliflower, cereals and milk. Things that men buy who don't know much about cooking. When we got back, the boys had left. Dennis and I laboured to make up a boiled sausage stew and then looked for the pub.

It was the first night of the show, but it was a work night in Bundaberg: a slow, sad, family night. The rides were turning, spinning, going up and down and around, each playing screeching, incoherent music, and the spruikers were working hard, badgering good-naturedly the few customers who wandered through sideshow alley. But there weren't many takers.

We found Mauler and Leroy drinking 4X in the outside garden area of a show-bar that looked onto bleachers built around the show-ring. I bought four beers, and settled on a seat beside Mauler, catching teasing glimpses of the show-ring between the bleachers where horse events and wood-chopping competitions were taking place. Every now and then, I wandered over to the edge of the ring to watch men dressed in white singlets and pants, hacking away with great speed at blocks of wood, or to gaze in the near distance at black-helmeted equestrians lifting their mounts over fences and hedges, raising small explosions of dust as they landed.

'Where are the Cherbourg boys?' I asked when I returned from one of my excursions.

'Amstering in,' Dennis answered with a chuckle, because he knew I wouldn't understand.

'What?'

'Getting free rides. That's what they call it, "amstering in". The showmen have lots of words like that. They speak a sort of backwards pig Latin with each other too when they don't want outsiders to understand them. You'll hear it.'

When Dennis finished schooling me he said, 'Brophy is going to be at Rockhampton.'

'Who told you that, Dennis?' Mauler asked, shocked.

'Michael,' Dennis answered, sipping his beer, looking at the townspeople who passed, but in such a way that he could still see Mauler from the corner of his eye. 'He heard it from Scourge.'

'Who's Brophy?' I asked.

'Fred Brophy,' Mauler answered me. 'He's got a boxing troupe too. I fought for him for a long time. Fred don't like me.' Mauler finished his beer in another gulp and lobbed the can into a rusted tin garbage drum. 'Wayne, you gonna buy another beer or what?'

'Buy your own, Mauler. How many boxing troupes are there?'

'Come on, Wayne, buy us a beer. We just poor Murris.'

'Leroy, I just bought you a beer. Get a sub from Michael if you haven't got any money.'

'Just Bell's and Brophy's,' said Dennis, answering my question, chuckling, getting up to buy a beer for himself and me, saying as he stood that if I wasn't careful Mauler and Leroy would have me buying all their beers.

Mauler followed him, coming back with two beers and a lit cigarette that he had bludged from somebody, giving one beer to Leroy and when Leroy demanded, sharing the cigarette with him.

Michael arrived at the bar angry. 'I'm not happy with the position we've got. Scourge could have done better. We're right down in a corner.'

I let Michael get a beer, blinking wildly, before I asked him about Brophy.

'Yeah, he's coming to Rockhampton, and Brophy's not even a show guild member,' Michael added angrily. 'His family have been around the show grounds for a long while, but he's got no boxing tent history. He tells everybody he has but . . .' Michael was still shaking his head in exasperation, when he added, 'The show society are paying him to be their attraction. We're not going to do any good in Rocky.'

47

'What's an attraction, mate?' I asked, realizing I didn't know half of what was going on.

'The show society pays for some act or exhibition they reckon might bring in more people to the show,' Michael answered abstractly. 'They're paying Brophy to put on a tent boxing show, and open it free to the public.'

Michael took another sip of beer and nodded his head to no one in particular. 'We're going to have to challenge them. Mauler, you're going to have to fight Cowboy.'

'What, he's their best fighter, he'll kill me,' Mauler said quickly, forcing the words together until they came out almost as a squeal.

'If he's got any other big blokes, I'll fight them,' Michael answered, disregarding Mauler's concerns. And then he walked into the bar and bought five new beers.

At times showmen ambled past. Most because business was slow and they had time on their hands. Many came over and shook Dennis's hand.

The next morning I was up before daylight. Dennis was already outside spooning instant coffee into a mug. The rest of our camp slept.

'Where you going, Little Fella?'

'Jogging.'

'Want some coffee first?'

'Love some,' I answered, before settling into one of the big, fake-leather chairs and wrapping myself in a towel against the morning cold. Dennis spooned coffee into another cup and waited patiently for the jug to boil. 'Is Cowboy that good?'

'Supposed to be, but I ain't never seen him fight. I know he's been fighting for Brophy for a long time.'

'How did Mauler end up with Brophy?' I asked, shivering.

'Brophy picked him up when he was living with a Walbiri woman up in Katherine in the Northern Territory. He lived with his in-laws and collected dole. He told me he was always drunk and broke, and the police were picking him up all the time, so when Brophy turned up, he went along with him, fighting all over the place.

'Little Fella, I've been thinking – ' But before Dennis could continue, the jug began to wheeze and then whistle loudly.

We sipped the sweet milky coffee, wrapping our hands around the mug to warm them, both blowing on the steaming drink to cool it.

'Do you remember fighting a Murri in Newcastle?' Dennis suddenly asked me.

'I remember everybody, except the bloke I fought in my second fight in Newcastle. I don't have a clue what his name was. He was taller and heavier, and he was dark, I remember that. But I thought he was a Greek or Italian.'

'A Wog,' Dennis said.

'Yeah, a Wog,' I answered. 'I know he already had thirty-odd fights.'

'Did he knock you out in the second round?'

'Near the end of the second. I was punching hell out of him, and then I walked into a big right hand. I got up and charged him, swinging away like a bloody amateur. It was the first time I had ever been down, and I reckon he must have hurt my feelings. Anyway, he caught me with another right hand.'

'I've always been like that, can't sit back and cover up when I've been hurt. Just like a bloody amateur. Do you know the ref came up after the fight and told me I was winning so easily that he thought about stopping the fight.' Dennis was looking at the ground, grinning. 'What are you getting at?'

'What year was it?'

'Nineteen seventy-four,' I answered not needing to stop and think, because it had been my first loss, and it had started my downward spiral in the fight game. I was to lose by way of knockout many more times after that.

'I fought Short's bloke in nineteen seventy-four. How many little blond-headed fellas were training with Short then?'

'Just me,' I answered.

That morning I ran along the banks of a deep brown river, one of those Australian waterways that only look substantial as they near the sea. Boats passed heading out to fish the ocean, sleek white things with lots of chrome and comfort. Rowing scuttles sped along the flat glass surface like tadpoles wriggling across a muddy waterhole. The rising sun glazed the waterway a dirty gold. When I got back, Dennis had already told the camp that he had knocked me out in 1974.

'Come on, Mikey, hurry up, we've got to get going.'

Michael called again before Mikey came out of the caravan still tying laces and doing up buttons on his school uniform.

The showmen had their own school. Two cleverly designed trailers that they used as classrooms. Two trucks to pull the trailers, and four teachers. All curriculum books and the latest computers. The showmen designed their own uniform. When Mikey was finally ready, Leroy offered to cook him eggs, but he left without eating.

'Good about the school,' I said to Michael as we drove into town to find Mauler and Leroy a new image, because the boxing tent was also about theatre.

'It's only been going about ten years. In my time we had to go to local schools. More fighting than learning. When we got to high school age we were sent away to board. A lot came back though, couldn't take the life away from the show. Plenty of showmen can't read or write.'

Michael gave me cash and sent me off with the Moree boys to get them a haircut. Shave them, was my order. The hairdresser, using electric clippers, left two millimetres on the top and one on the sides. They came out looking like marines.

Michael bought Leroy a pair of white training shoes and dark-coloured, lightweight tracksuit pants. To outfit Mauler, we had to go to an army disposal store. Michael bought him camouflage pants, khaki singlets, an army belt and desert boots.

'Forget Moree Mauler,' Michael said, turning to face him as he came out of the fitting room. 'Your new name is Russian Rambo. You're an Afghanistan war veteran.'

Mauler rubbed his hand across his shaven head and flexed his muscles, looking into a full-sized mirror at his new clothes. All he said was 'Rambo eh?' and for the first time, I noticed the large tattooed goanna crawling up his arm towards a fish inked over a badly scarred bicep.

'And what about me, Michael, who am I?'

'Leroy, you're the camp cook, been with us twenty years. We carry you along to fight all the old fellas who still want to have a go, or for the young fellas who don't have much experience. All right?'

'You the boss, Michael, I just hope I don't let you down.'

All afternoon, Mauler and Leroy sat drinking in the bar. When I passed, I asked Mauler how he expected to fight drunk. 'I can't fight sober,' he said to me. 'Brophy would always give me money to drink before I had to fight.'

'Why doesn't Brophy like you now?' I asked, sitting with them, thinking it unlikely Brophy gave him money to drink, but finally relenting and buying them a beer anyway.

'I ran off once, had enough, didn't want to fight any more.

51

Anyway, Brophy don't like Murris, reckons we're undependable.' Mauler pronounced the word syllable by syllable. 'I don't want to fight Cowboy though. Cowboy'll kill me.'

'Have you ever seen him fight?' I asked.

'No,' Mauler answered, 'never even seen him.'

When I returned from the bar, Dennis and I laid down the canvas boxing mat in its correct position between the king poles. First filling in any holes and levelling the ground out as best we could with sawdust. We then hammered in light pegs around the mat, pulled the mat up, and laid down strips of horsehair padding, finally repositioning the mat over the padding and stretching and tying it down one corner at a time until we had a taut surface. Making sure the pegs were in deep and completely covered with earth.

Michael supervised, checking the rope ties, and dancing on the mat to test its firmness. Then he slept, readying himself for his night's work. When he woke, he sent me to look for Mauler and Leroy. The Cherbourg boys had already returned after a day of amstering in, and were eating the dregs out of the pot of sausage stew, not bothering to use plates, mopping the pot out with day-old white bread.

The crowd was different from the first day, less families. Groups of youths moved quickly and erratically through sideshow alley. It was a Friday night crowd, a better one for us, for everybody.

I found Mauler and Leroy still at the bar. From the show-ring came the high-pitched squeal of dirt motorbikes. At times, lit up by the powerful lights, I would catch sight of them flying through the air, but how they landed I couldn't tell, only that it was without mishap, because the applause was always immense, and you don't clap for crashes.

*

We waited when we got back, Michael was not satisfied, the crowd was not big enough. Mauler and Leroy sat inside the trailer rolling joints from the yanni they had bought during the day for twenty bucks a cone.

'How can you tell?' I asked, convinced that we should be up on the board getting the show started.

'It's experience,' Michael said patiently, 'and I always look at the Ferris wheel. When that's full, we've got enough mugs to put on a show.' It was the first time I had heard Michael call the crowd mugs.

'Another thing,' he continued, 'it's hard work spruiking a crowd into the tent, and when you don't have enough paying mugs, you're just wasting your men. It's got to be just right. Most people don't understand that.'

It was only a short while later that Michael told Dennis and myself to put the drum and bell onto the line-up board, and get the boys dressed. And while we did, Michael started his pre-fight patter.

'Ladies and gentlemen, tonight there's going to be plenty of boxing spills and wrestling thrills for Bell's cash prizes. We're just getting ready for the big opening session, so stick around, boys.'

People stopped immediately. It was as if a fence had suddenly appeared to bale them up. Newcomers milled like sheep, refusing to pass. The joints near the tent were surrounded with people, their business temporarily finished.

Dennis and I unloaded the big metal trunk full of gowns and boxing trunks, and then the other filled with gloves, boots and headgear from the back of the trailer, and carried them inside the tent. The different coloured boxing gowns, most rumpled and cordless, were tipped along with the boxing trunks onto the mat where Dennis and I handed them out as if they were uniforms for extras in a film.

After the boys were dressed, they moved around the tent like caged cats, while Dennis stood in a corner, opening and closing his hands in a boxer's spasm, and when he thought people weren't looking, throwing heavy punches at the air.

'Wayne, Wayne,' Michael called down from the line-up board. 'Get dressed, I want you on the drum. Send Dennis out here to keep control of the ladder.'

I changed quickly into boxing trunks, draped a gown over my shoulders, and went out through the tent entrance. Scourge and a slight, pretty, dark-haired woman who I learnt was his wife Leanne were standing just outside the doorway, money aprons strapped around their waists. I climbed the ladder that Dennis now guarded like a junkyard dog against the gangs of unrestrained youth gathered in front of the tent.

'Dah d-dah d-dah d-dah, you got it?' Michael asked, as he finished tapping on the metal drum casing. When I nodded, he yelled down to send Leroy up to ring the bell. Our duet began in earnest . . . Boom ba boom ba boom ba boom.

'Send up Chris and Zac,' Michael yelled to Dennis over the banging and the ringing.

When the two boys stood on the board, hands crossed modestly in front of them, looking over the heads of the crowd that was growing and growing, Michael whistled sharply. 'Hold da, hold da, hold da.' And we stopped banging and ringing as if we'd been shot.

'Come up here, Jail Break,' Michael called to Zac. 'This young fella is on the run.' . . . 'Shake 'em up, shake 'em up,' . . . Boom ba boom ba boom. The crowd fidgeted. Then the whistle and the 'Hold da, hold da,' and in the comparative stillness, Michael told the crowd about the dangerous history of Street Fighter, who was just a boy from Cherbourg called Chris . . . Then he told them about Leroy the Camp Cook, who had been with the troupe for twenty years, and who was carried along to fight any old fellas who wanted to have a go, or any young fella just starting out.

'Ladies and gentlemen,' Michael began again after more drums and bells, in a voice suddenly flushed with awe. 'Ladies and gentlemen, bare in mind, it always pays to carry along a man capable of knocking out anyone along the length and breadth of Australia, and tonight I have with my troupe a man who can do just that. Send out the Russian Rambo.'

Mauler, dressed in his battle fatigues, came rushing out, squinting, scowling, and carrying a heavy crowbar menacingly.

'Here he is, ladies and gentlemen. You've read about him in *People*, you've read about him in the *Post*, you've seen him on TV. He's straight from the front lines of the Afghanistan war. He's shell shocked, he's mean, he's dangerous.'

'Rambo, mark out the pitch,' Michael called down to him.

When Mauler drew a line in the dirt with the crowbar, the crowd drew back. The pitch had been marked.

And while Mauler danced awkwardly on the uneven ground, throwing big intimidating punches towards the crowd, Michael told us to shake it up, and I banged as loudly as I could until I heard the whistle and the 'Hold da, hold da.'

'Rambo, come up here and let them have a good look at ya.' Michael turned back to the crowd. 'Now, any one of you fighting men about town looking for a go at our star performer, or any of our other fighters, put your hands up.'

And they did. Tentatively, but with the regularity of a chronic dripping tap. Some had to be goaded by mates before they would come forward, others just climbed the ladder as if nothing could be more important on that warm winter night amidst the bellowing sounds and garish colours of the show grounds than to stand in front of their own people and show they had some mettle.

Michael worked them, encouraging when he noticed that someone was almost ready, spruiking the imaginary histories of our fighters one more time. Dennis moved amongst them using his own persuasion. They were not a difficult crowd and soon Michael had enough.

But they were all young, no big men; it was as if a generation was missing. There was nobody who could take on Mauler.

'Now get your tickets, ladies and gentlemen. The fights are just about to start.' Michael told the boys to get down from the line-up board, and spread out amongst the customers crowding into the tent. 'And watch the tent flaps, make sure nobody sneaks under them.'

'I want you to referee,' Michael said to me as I laid the big drum carefully onto the boards and moved towards the ladder. 'I'll be on the microphone calling the fights from below.' Michael pointed to a chair behind the side wall that allowed him a vantage over the whole tent. 'Just listen to what I'm saying.'

The crowds who paid ten dollars entrance fee were not big that first evening, but they were vocal and uneasy. You couldn't expect them to remain calm and impartial when their mates and townspeople were in the ring representing their worth.

A lot of the showmen came to watch. The younger ones moved amongst the crowd, helping the boxers keep control and working the corners: lacing gloves, slaking thirst, moping away sweat and blood, giving unsolicited advice. Without them, there wouldn't have been enough of us.

The matches were classless and tasteless. The Bundaberg boys came out to fight charging forward, bent over, swinging like windmill blades. Sometimes Zac and Chris had their hands full, but they were both good boxers and kept their punches straight enough to hold the storm at bay.

Leroy was stiff and awkward, but moved around well enough considering his age, and the alcohol and yanni inside him.

Michael kept the rounds short, careful that nobody got hurt, save for a few bruises and a little blood. He made sure that the locals received due praise, and kept the crowd part of the action and under control: 'No swearing here, there's women and children in the crowd, give the local boy a hand, make sure that fighters' all right, Wayne.'

He laughed loudly when I was forced to wrestle someone to the ground to stop him from lifting a knee in Chris's face, and at the innumerable times that wild punches missed me by fractions.

We had three houses that night, but they were all poor. Young fellas don't have much money after the drinking and the yanni.

'Not like in my day, then they was real fighters, Little Fella,' Dennis said, as we packed away the gloves and gowns into the chests and lifted down the drum and the bell from the line-up board before the instruments disappeared into the night. 'But things'll be different the further north we get, lot of big Islanders up there.'

Michael was stoic : 'It'll get better. I'm glad we got the first night over. Still not happy with our position though.' And then he asked us to go and drink a beer with him.

That night was my first time in 'the Hole in the Wall', the showmen's bar. Just sheets of canvas set between trucks, two large Eskies full of beer, and rum and Scotch mixes, and a few scattered stools. Payment was by honour system.

A large television had been hooked up because an important rugby league game was in progress. The bar, run by and exclusively for showmen, was impossible to find if you didn't know where to look. That evening there were no women present.

The swearing and the coarseness bothered me. It was like being amongst a clannish family that couldn't get on and didn't care who knew. Michael introduced me as a friend, and because Michael was part of their family, and because he was the hardest man in the bar, some softened towards me. But I was under no illusions, I knew I had no place amongst them.

When a showman told me I was only tolerated because I was with Michael, I knew exactly where I stood. This was a showmen's bar and I was not a showman, so be it.

Dennis was treated as an honoured guest. 'I knocked the Little Fella out,' I overheard him telling a young man with a fighter's nose and a movie star's smile, who was listening respectfully to his much repeated stories of old victories.

Mauler had already told me that Dennis had knocked me out fifty times that day. But I knew Dennis never meant a cruelty by telling the story, it had simply become part of his repertoire. An incident from his days of glory. Besides, I didn't think Dennis had any more cruelty in him.

When he was young, he told me, he would go around looking for white men to bash. He bashed plenty. 'I hated them before I started travelling in the boxing tent with Michael's pop and nanna. They treated me good, like a real person, made me like white people.' Dennis dropped his head momentarily as if looking for something that had fallen. 'They was good people, Little Fella. Yeah, travelling with the tent took the murder out of me. I mean that,' he added, when he saw my disbelieving look.

To be truthful, I was comforted to know that it was Dennis who had knocked me out that first time. Even proud, because I knew now that at least I was beaten by a renowned tent fighter, and because at one stage in the fight, I had him beaten. I didn't care who he told, actually he was doing me a favour, because anybody who fought Dennis as a professional must have been somebody. And to be somebody on the showgrounds helped.

*

Mikey looked frail standing on the line-up board in his red satin gown. He had lost weight in the week we had been travelling. Michael introduced him to the crowd as the schoolboy champion of Australia. Mikey was the next generation of tent fighters, the future of Bell's boxing tent. That was Michael's hope anyway. That would be most fathers' hope.

'Come up here, son. Let that little bloke through.' And when a small blond-headed fellow climbed the ladder, Mikey had his first opponent. It was a terrific fight, because they both were. They skidded around the mat as if it were ice and they were born with skates instead of feet, blocking and punching cleanly and with more skill than I had seen in two nights of tent fighting. Mikey had been well schooled and if it were me deciding, he would have won the fight. His father called it a draw. The crowd threw forty dollars into the ring.

Another boy called Knuckles fought that second night. I had met his father the same day in a bar where he was happily buying beers for Mauler and Leroy and supplying them with Marlboro cigarettes. It was his crushing handshake that I remember most. A natural grip, well timed, sincere. He wanted us to take Knuckles along on the run.

'He's a good kid and he can fight. I want you to make something of him.' It was a request from a proud father, not someone worried that his son was on the wrong track. Nor from a dad who couldn't handle his son and wanted to transfer the responsibility.

After he finished telling me this, I gazed ahead, seeing nothing because my thoughts had overwhelmed my sight and temporarily blinded me. It happened often and sometimes I thought it might be the first signs of a disease. Mauler lobbed another empty beer can in the rusted garbage drum in front of the bar. It rattled loudly as it landed, waking me like the click of a hypnotist's fingers.

'You sleeping?' Mauler yelled at me in the high-pitched voice he used when he was excited or drunk or unsure. I shook my head to clear it.

'Buy us a beer.'

'Come on, Waynee,' Leroy said, adding an extra e to my name, as he liked doing, something I usually didn't like, wouldn't allow, but from Leroy didn't mind, because it wasn't meant as an insult.

I ordered four 4X beers, thinking again about the request from Knuckles' father, but this time aware of my company, listening with one ear to more talk of prisons, screws, black gangs, white gangs, stand-over merchants.

Why would he want to send his son to fight with us, I thought to myself. It seemed so old-fashioned. He should be thinking about an education or a steady job for the boy. I wouldn't know any fathers who would want to send their sixteen-year-old boys away to be a tent fighter these days.

Then I remembered that Dennis had told me it was the best thing that ever happened to him. But that was a time when Dennis had nothing. Also I was not shocked that Zac and Chris wanted to travel with us, or that Zac's mother gave permission. And they were only seventeen.

But I knew what it was: Dennis, Chris and Zac had all made their own decision to travel with the tent. Neither Dennis nor the boys needed parental encouragement.

Another thing, Knuckles was white. Unfairly, he had so many more advantages than the Cherbourg boys, so many more choices. It was not supposed to be like that, but it was. Dennis, Mauler, Leroy: they had made that clear to me.

Knuckles fought twice that night. He was raw, untrained, but strong and hard like his father claimed him to be. Michael offered to take him.

*

'Ladies and gentlemen, this will be the last fight of the night, and we call it the grudge match. This is your chance to get back at the bloke who stole your girlfriend, or the one who kicked your dog.' But there were no gentlemen nor ladies left in the crowd. To the martial sound of the bell and the drum, Michael matched mates against mates.

The friends fought with passionate vigour, unrestrained fierceness. Every one of them. They were perilous to referee, and any onlooker who stood too close to the unroped ring risked being crushed or hit, or drawn into the melee.

Our boxers had their hands full keeping out young Aboriginal boys who rolled under the tent flaps like grains of dark sand in a willy-willy. There were screams of 'Kill him, kill him,' 'Rip his fucking head off.' These came from the girlfriends, sisters and mothers.

When the police came to watch the last of the fights, a scurry of movement under the tent flaps began again. This time it was people who needed to leave in a hurry.

We had just finished putting away the boxing gear, when a worker from the food canteen across the alley turned up with uneaten Pluto Pups and chips smothered in tomato sauce. Mauler, who had only fought once that night, against a slow, overweight biker who had collapsed through lack of oxygen in the second round, sat contentedly rolling a joint, still fingering ketchup that remained in one of the empty paper chip cups, licking his fingers loudly, smearing the smoke paper red.

Although there was little noise, save for the occasional maniacal shriek or obscene scream from a showground that had shut down for the night, nobody heard the copper walk into our camp. He was tall, fit, as broad as Mauler, high cheekbones, clean cut: black.

'You see a Murri kid with his hair pulled back in a ponytail around here?' he asked Mauler. But he had the wrong man. Mauler wouldn't give his own people away, the copper should have known that. Mauler looked up slowly, as surprised to see the copper as everyone. He stared, disregarding the question, asking his own in his excited voice squeal. 'Hey, what's your name, brother?'

The copper looked angrily down at Mauler, but if Mauler noticed you couldn't tell because he continued staring, waiting for an answer. Surprisingly the police officer seemed to relax. He folded his arms and smiled with perfect teeth. 'Jackson,' he finally said.

'Hey, you know the Moree Jacksons?'

'I have an uncle in Moree.'

'Then we from the same mob. We's cousins,' he said, excited.

Mobs, I was learning, were Mauler's specialty. Any time he would come across another Murri he would always ask his name, checking if there was any mob affiliation. The officer and Mauler had just started discussing families, when I noticed the joint that Mauler continued to roll. I kicked him lightly on the leg and then harder, which caught the copper's attention at the same time it caught Mauler's. The two men from the same mob stared stupidly at the joint, before the officer looked towards the sky as if suddenly enamoured with the light grey clouds that the warm breeze had shunted above us, cleared his throat, and said, 'Better get after the little bastard.' And he was gone.

We slowly crept to our cots in dribs and drabs, exhausted, our first show finished.

When I got up to piss, the same grey clouds were dropping misting rain. The aviation warning lights mounted on the Ferris wheel and Big Drop blinked nervously through the chilly murkiness. Unmoving rides towered menacingly above the gaudy joints. It was mercifully quiet.

I was returning to the truck when I heard the moan, delicate and continuous. In the noiselessness it was easy to recognize. Mauler had her pressed up against the Kenworth. Folds of her blonde hair draped over Mauler's shoulder as he nuzzled her neck. It was the girl from the last house, the one standing with the group of Aboriginal women. She could have been Aboriginal herself, you couldn't tell these days. I didn't linger.

The next morning, Dennis and I were drinking coffee when Michael walked into the damp, clammy camp.

'Where are the boys?'

'Still sleeping,' Dennis answered, 'you won't get Mauler and Leroy up until you kick them. They were drinking pretty heavy last night.'

'You've got to keep them under control a bit, that's your job. You're the camp boss.'

'They don't listen to me, Michael, especially Leroy. A few easy bouts against kids who can't fight, and all of a sudden he thinks he's a big tent boxer. Sometimes he makes me pretty mad.' Dennis had his large hands squeezed tightly together, he was leaning forward in his chair looking towards the ground, his brown hair fell in cascades across his face.

Michael was about to rouse the boys when he stopped, turned and pulled a chair up next to us. 'Got another coffee?'

I made him some and asked, 'How did we do?'

'Earned enough to pay for the ground and food, that's about it. I wanted to send some money back to Mandy, but that'll have to wait. We should do better as we head further north.'

'I thought you had to pay Scourge. Doesn't he own the ground?'

'It's got nothing to do with the deal I made with Scourge. He has the right to use it, but he doesn't own it. It's still got to be paid for.'

'I don't understand,' I said, dropping two pieces of white bread in the toaster. 'Anybody want toast?' I asked, piling up more pieces of bread ready. 'Well?' I asked.

'A showmen's guild was formed years ago, it's sort of like our union. Anyway, Michael continued slowly, carefully, 'the guild's bosses made an agreement with the local show societies who control all the showgrounds in Australia to give a part of the show grounds for use by the sideshows at each Show. The guild bosses then divided up and allocated the ground to the show families. Sometimes they did it by drawing lots to make it fairer, but mostly they just handed them out willy nilly. But the families still have to pay the show societies for the ground. You understand?' I nodded.

'Everything's worked out in feet. Sometimes you've got to pay a dollar a foot, sometimes, depending where you're showing, it can be eight dollars a foot.

'Our guild has maps of all the ground on all the showgrounds, and you can get a copy, but not many bother because they have it in their heads, or think they do. Sometimes there are disputes, because families can't get a machine in here or a joint in there, and then the arguments begin. Some of them are beauties,' Michael added . . . whistling.

'Don't you have any ground?' I asked him.

'The Bells do, but Dad was left out of all that. To tell you the truth, I was hoping they would see their way clear to letting me use some. Most of their ground is on the Darwin run. That would have worked out better I reckon. A lot more travelling up bush, but they're not as spoilt for entertainment like the mugs here on the North run, and they love the boxing tent.'

'But that didn't happen?'

'No, that's why I made the deal with Scourge. Usually he got his house of mirrors on his ground, but he can earn more with me.'

We had done eating when the two Cherbourg boys appeared, rubbing their eyes and scratching different parts of their bodies.

Michael jumped up, leapt inside the trailer and shook Mauler and Leroy by their feet. 'Get up, we've got to pull down and get out of here.'

Without giving them time to eat, we started taking apart the line-up board, folding the banners with exaggerated care, dismantling the loudspeakers, loosening tent ropes, pulling down the side walls, and dropping the poles.

When only the four corner poles were left, the Cherbourg boys were sent into the heart of the tent to pull at the feet of the king poles and extract them as if they were splinters being pulled from flesh. The tent collapsed, curtseying like a schoolgirl meeting the queen.

Mauler was set to work banging at the pegs with the sledgehammer, while Leroy loosened them from the ground. One hit each side . . . pull, and they were free. The rest of us hauled the fake leather chairs to the top of the truck, dropped the punching bag from its hoist, packed away tables, toasters, jugs, dirty plates and mugs, pulled down the camp tarpaulin, and dug up the mat.

There was an order to loading, but discipline and experience were needed and we had neither. Michael stood on the back of the truck, loading and yelling: the tent pegs, the entrance gates, now the line-up boards, now the . . . He wanted it to be perfect, to work like clockwork, just like his pop did it. I could understand, but that would take time.

Knuckles told us that he would be at our camp and ready to travel before we finished pulling down. He didn't show up, and we never saw him again.

GIN GIN

When we drove out of town towards Gin Gin it was still morning. We followed Michael, who was part of a small convoy of showmen's trucks. The larger rides and many of the joints had moved on to Gladstone, the next big town up the coast. Gin Gin was a small show, there just wasn't enough money to go round. The Moree boys drove with me.

As we passed through the suburbs of Bundaberg, Mauler, his head hanging out of the window and a cigarette drooping from his mouth, spotted Aboriginals everywhere.

'Hey, this place is full of Murris,' he said to no one, confident, like a man who's discovered he's not alone in a strange place. Some he would tell us reminded him of family members, of mates or old girlfriends. At times he would yell, 'Hey, brother/Hey, sister, what's your name?' Sure that they were from the same mob. Leroy always haughtily agreed with his pronouncements, as if between the two of them, no Murri from their mob could ever hope to escape their notice.

'I could have knocked you out anytime, Little Fella. In those days, I was sparring all the time with Tony Mundine. I was just playing with you for a couple of rounds, letting you hit me. Me and Tony even used to double date. We was good mates, Little Fella.'

I smiled and nodded when Dennis said this, concentrating on the road, checking every now and then that the caravan still clung to the Ford. I had become used to Dennis's promulgations, and I felt bad for him that he had never reached the heights in the professional fight game that he deserved, sure that I had him beat that night.

Dennis's reminiscence started me thinking about the world title fight Tony Mundine had with the great Argentinean middleweight Carlos Monzon. Monzon knocked out Tony, but had in later life become nothing more than a common murderer after he threw his wife to her death from a window, while Tony had become a respected and loved man.

We were still travelling through land suffocated by cane, passing houses that were all but smothered by the crop, and then the country began to climb in earnest, and suddenly we were in cattle country.

A stand of dead eucalyptus trees stood on a hillock outside of the town like a macabre warning, but then a neat sign just before the town limits claimed that Gin Gin was the friendliest place in Queensland.

We put up the line-up board, banners and tent in the oppressing midday heat, not unpacking all of the camp, because the next day we would be off to Gladstone. We ate show food, washed clothes, rested.

In the cool of the afternoon, I walked around the showground that was hemmed in on one side by the small town and on the other by cattle country. The ring was its essence, its showplace for great beasts, the stage for unparalleled horsemen and woodchoppers. There were lots of home-baked and homemade things to judge. Sideshow alley was a small diversion. It was an old-fashioned show, a family one according to Scourge. We shouldn't expect to do too good.

When I got back to the tent, I pulled out the punching mitts and offered to give the boys some training. Michael had not schooled anyone so far, and I thought I could help.

I was trying to straighten up Mauler's punches, get him to move around, use more straight lefts, make it easy on himself, when Michael came in and took over.

I watched from the side of the mat as he dismissed Mauler, and told the Cherbourg boys to lace on gloves. 'Hold your hands high,' he instructed them, 'watch your opponents closely, let them throw the punches, cover up, they'll wear themselves out. Push them back, come over with hooks.

'If you're getting beat,' he continued, 'walk off the mat, the ref will stop it. If he's a mug and walks off the mat, keep throwing punches,' but then added: 'If he's all right, leave him alone. Learn where the dips and holes are in the mat. You choose where to fight. Don't worry, I'm watching, I won't let anybody get hurt.'

It was an effective fighting technique designed to fight out of condition brawlers and drunks. It had little to do with professional boxing: no real footwork, no ropes to work off, straight lefts, lateral movements were superfluous. It was quick action, just what the public wanted.

'Do you think he'll turn up?' Michael asked. He was talking to a short, wide man whose lower arms were broad and erratically covered with veins that put me in mind of ink-blue rivers gushing into an estuary.

'He'll turn up, mugs like that always do.'

I knew then that Michael was talking to a showman. 'What's up?' I asked after the man had left.

'Some bastard pissed on one of our caravans last year. It took two of our blokes to handle him. If he comes tonight, I want him fighting in the tent. A bloke like that can pull the crowd in.'

He was spotted in the early evening, walking through the grounds with a mate. He was big, towering over everybody and, if the sun was just right, shading them. His mate was small only in comparison. It was like watching an elephant sauntering next to a hippopotamus.

We had set up the tent in sight of the bar that had been erected in an open-sided shed with planks and barrels. Work solid men, with faces seared and grooved by unrelenting sun and wind, stood around it drinking beer and Bundaberg rum.

They were dressed in hip-length wool-lined jackets and crushed and faded Akubra hats. All wore elastic-sided riding boots. There were women, but only of the type that can sit a prancing horse or herd a cow. The drinkers, like most people standing in their own house amongst their own kind, were loud, confident and gracious.

We stood on the board exposed to a cold, cutting wind, stepping from foot to foot, looking over a small crowd. The drum banged away, leading the bell in an unsophisticated duet, interrupting the cattlemen's conversation, causing a restlessness. Intriguing but not tempting them.

'Hold da, hold da, this is Bell's touring boxing stadium, where they fight and where they wrestle.' And then Michael's steel sharp whistle slashed through the drumbeat. 'Stick around, boys, we're here to take on all comers . . . it's barred to no man.'

Michael was looking at the big fellow when he said this, silently challenging him, leaving him the chance to come forward or decline with no loss of face. Without warning, the hippopotamus, who had been standing at his mate's side pushed through the crowd and climbed unsteadily up to the line-up board.

We thought he wanted to fight. The bar noise dropped to a murmur and then to nothing as the wind gusted, carrying it away, and, for the first time that evening, only the screeching, mangled music from the rides could be heard.

The hippopotamus reached for the microphone, but released it when Michael gave him a quiet warning. It only became obvious what he wanted when he signalled his big mate to come on up.

Agonizing, farcical moments passed as the hippopotamus bounced on the boards, gesturing wildly. The big fellow stood where he was, uncomfortably hunched, smiling stupidly, wanting no part of it. Finally Michael asked hippopotamus: 'Why don't you fight?'

Both the elephant and the hippopotamus looked like they had reached thirty, and were dressed as if the town were just a crossroads on the way to somewhere more sophisticated. Their haircuts were city. It seemed to me that they had nothing to do with the land around them, the beasts that supported the town economically, the people who gave it its character and proclaimed hospitality.

In them I recognized schoolboy bullies. It was always the same: a big one and one who felt big because he was under protection. They were of the type that always proved gutless when the odds were equal, but could be disturbingly cruel when they weren't. I heard later that the elephant and hippopotamus were lawyers, and that the big fella was a stand-over merchant.

Refusing Michael's offer, the hippopotamus climbed arrogantly back down the ladder, as if we were the fools on this cold country evening.

Michael had to fight that night. A tiny drunk man challenged him. Michael tried to dissuade him, and when he found that he couldn't, agreed to fight him, but made it clear to everyone that while the little man could fight standing, he would fight from his knees.

'You can't refuse a fight if it's your business, it'll give the tent a bad reputation,' Michael whispered to me, covering the microphone with one hand, leaning his hand lightly on the drum to steady himself, making it heavier to hold than it already was. 'Don't worry, I won't hurt him.'

'Hurt him. If the little bastard can fight, he's going to be hard to keep off.' Michael smiled wryly, showing his teeth like a dog who'd eaten bad food.

It was a risk fighting on your knees, but the little man was what he seemed, a small, sweet drunk who couldn't fight. Michael gave him a couple of hard thumps because this was a boxing tent, but he allowed the little man to leave with money, under the roar of approval from his townsfolk.

Mauler had to fight as well. Earlier in the evening, I was approached by a man and woman who claimed family to one of Australia's greatest fighters, Les Darcy. Knowing we needed a big man to draw any sort of crowd, I did my best to talk him into fighting Mauler. I promised that Mauler would take it easy, and used his family bloodline as an argument as to why he could not refuse.

'He ain't a Darcy,' his wife spat at me, 'I'm a Darcy. Ya gunna get him hurt, ya mongrel.'

But the idea had settled in the man's mind and anybody who has ever been on the board, or heard the drum, could understand the turmoil of his decision.

'I'll have a go,' he finally said, not looking at his wife, dancing up and down, swinging his arms to loosen them like someone who fights each week

'You bastard. If he gets hurt, I'm gunna kill ya.'

'We'll look after him,' I promised again, bringing only a look of disdain on her face.

I refereed the fight, reminding Mauler at every clinch not to hurt the man, flinching when Mauler forgot himself and let fly with haymakers that would have made the woman a widow if they had landed.

He finished the fight with swelling around one eye, and a small loss of blood, enough to elicit another 'Look at his face, ya mongrel,' from the wife. The man himself was all smiles because he had just gone three rounds with the Russian Rambo, and the crowd was cheering, and how often does that happen in your life? I paid his earnings to his wife, with a 'Ya mongrel, he could have been killed,' as thanks.

The Cherbourg boys had it tough as usual, battling the wild youth of Australia, but Leroy showed some style in his fight. His opponent was inexperienced, but he did it easy. Another thing, he was coughing and spitting less.

Dennis and I had become close. We were reminders to each other of the days when we were the best we could be, and it's always good to be reminded. After the show we wandered over to a concert of country music, performed by a tall middle-aged man wearing shit-kicker boots and a black American-style cowboy hat. They had set up a small stage for him, and placed benches in front, running back towards the bar.

The cold had become painful, and the non-drinkers who sat on the benches seemed to drop down into their coats like snails seeking sanctum in the frailty of their shells, leaving as little as they could exposed to the wind that seemed to belong to a different continent. Dennis and I stood near the benches because we wanted to listen to the music without the intrusive roars and whelps from the bar drinkers.

'Beer's warmer than the weather, Little Fellow.' Dennis's words were shrouded in vapour and soft, so that the sounds of the song rolled over them like an ocean swell.

An old man, unshaven and with eyelids folded over like silk

drapes, turned and faced us. 'We usta have forty-four gallon drums placed all over the paddock with fires burning in them to keep us warm. Didn't have to sit on benches like frozen garden gnomes. But these days the show society is worried about some idiot scorching himself and suing, and there is always some mongrel lawyer that knows just how to do that. We're getting more like America every day. Can't do any bloody thing any more.' Dennis grunted his agreement.

'Too right,' continued the old man, as if just speaking kept him warm. 'Kids' sports teams have folded because the injury insurance is too high. Parks have closed because parents sue the council every time little Jonny grazes a knee. No drinking, no smoking, no fires. The country's gone bloody mad. Don't let anybody ever tell you we're free out here.'

I felt a sudden surge of disappointment, and the thought that maybe I had left it too long to return rushed through me. Dennis and I persevered with our warm beers on the cold evening, listening to that sweet music. It was a good night, a family show, an illusion.

'Go and find Mauler. There's going to be trouble.' I hadn't noticed Michael until he was whispering in my ear. Mauler was not to be found.

The hippopotamus had pissed in our tent. Michael couldn't let this go. The showmen protected their ground with ferocity; it was the closest thing they had to a home. It was a drunken juvenile challenge, an attempt to emulate his big mate who had pissed on a showman's caravan the year before. It was a mistake.

Michael gave him a chance to apologize, to walk away, and he almost did. Perhaps it was because the bar was looking on, or that his mate was standing near him. In any case a temporary bravado took hold, harsh, foul words spewed from his mouth, his face twisted into a comical grimace and he swung. It was a weak effort, easy to block, and Michael needed only a left hook, and a straight right, to put him on the ground.

When the Elephant reached for Michael, I was next to him. I could see his face, he had no intention of fighting, only of saving peace; he was frightened. When I moved to grab him, I was knocked to the ground by four showmen who came over the top of me, fists flying.

It was a committed, merciless attack, and the big fellow was felled in seconds. His great weight left him struggling to rise like an overfed boar. When he finally stood, Michael asked him if he wanted to continue. 'Just me,' Michael made it clear, but there was no fight in him.

The crowd had moved away from the bar to get a better view. Michael screamed out loud enough for them to hear that the two men had pissed in his boxing tent. And then I thought it was over.

All I noticed was a quick unprovoked movement, a swirl of long hair, and the flash of gold, that could have been a ring or a knuckleduster. The punches, thrown only by one man, were aimed at the side of the big fellow's head, and came from behind.

The big fellow took five hard rights thrown with powerful precision before he went down again. This time he got up more slowly, and stood unsteadily, one side of his face a dreadful mask of red. Eyelid skin lifting up and over one eye. The showmen disappeared almost magically. I looked towards the bar, turned back to the mayhem, and they were gone.

Dennis, who had been standing behind me, tapped me lightly on the shoulder. 'Come on, Little Fella, this is not our way,' and we moved back towards the music, which seemed to offer sanctity in its brotherly tones.

Later in the evening, Michael slipped quietly up behind us

again, staying in the shadows. He was almost unrecognizable. His plait had been slipped underneath a black woollen cap, and his blue satin jacket had been replaced by an old black jumper.

'I think they've called the police, they haven't been off their telephones, we've been watching them. It's either the coppers or mates, but I don't think they have many mates. If it is the cops, you don't know anything.'

'We don't talk to coppers, Michael, you know that.'

Michael nodded when Dennis said this, blinking wildly, making himself appear a little mad.

'You know I had to hook him,' he said to me, breathing heavily.

'He deserved it,' I answered, 'no two ways about it.'

This seemed to comfort Michael because he began to nod his head slowly, and then I said, 'But I didn't like the way the big bastard was king hit.'

'Neither did I. Dad always said it's a better victory if you fight fair. I wanted to keep it from getting out of control, that's why I yelled out that the mongrel had pissed in our tent. I wanted them blokes at the bar to understand the reason for the fight. I thought they might back up the mongrels. If anybody asks, tell them we are heading off to Charters Towers.' I nodded, knowing that Charters Towers was around 1,000 kilometres north-east of our next destination.

Four coppers turned up within minutes and Michael was gone. You could see them moving around, stopping men, asking questions, moving on and stopping more. Dennis and I moved back into the darkness as they passed near us heading towards our truck. The country music continued in the frosty air.

We heard later that when Michael spotted the coppers coming towards the truck, he told Leroy to piss on the boxing tent mat. 'Then get rid of the yanni, find a copper and shown him the stain.'

The original despoiling had dried, leaving only a light smear that could be mistaken for a scuff mark.

The coppers never found Michael, nor the showmen, and when they questioned any of our mob, they were told nothing. Michael had been morally and legally in the right but it was always better to say nothing, especially when lawyers were involved. Besides, there was always the questions that could arise about the way the big fellow was king hit. For Michael, there was nothing more important than protecting the tent, and that also meant protecting it from delays. And any sort of police attention would certainly bring them.

The Gin Gin coppers persisted in their search, but it was hard for them on that dark cold night because the man they were looking for, the amber-skinned, long-haired fighter wearing a blue satin jacket had vanished.

I asked Dennis what could have happened to Mauler. 'Mauler don't like fighting, Little Fella, he was probably hiding somewhere. He's been in a lot of trouble . . . He don't mean it, you see what he's like. There's nothing bad in him, just sometimes too much drinking and women, and people like to have a go at him.

'I don't know whether he told you this, but he head butted a fella into a coma up in Kununurra one time. A fella from another mob. The bloke was swearing at his girlfriend, calling her all sorts of things. He's been in jail a few times too for bashing blokes. It's just the drink. I think he's scared to hurt people. He don't like to fight too much now.'

Dennis and I decided on one last drink. The country singer had started another set, but the crowd had dwindled. We wandered to the bar, towards the warmth given off by the other drinkers. We thought the trouble had finished. The police lingered, but they stood chatting contentedly amongst the town drinkers, the purpose of their presence lost to them in the futility of their search.

The big bloke charged at me out of nowhere, towering over me, staying just out of range. Frothing, screaming almost incoherently, accusing me of king hitting him. His mate turned up. But I had Dennis, and again the odds were not on their side. The crowd pushed between us, and the coppers finally arrived.

Michael had us up before light, pulling down the tent, intent on getting the hell out of town before the coppers returned. I took Leroy, hooked on the caravan, called the Cherbourg boys, and headed back to Bundaberg.

They had done what they had promised Michael, fought as hard as they could, now it was time to put them on a bus to Brisbane. Michael drove off in the opposite direction towards Gladstone, hoping he had left the trouble behind. The boys mumbled a quiet thanks when I paid them, keeping close to each other as they had the whole trip. They were tough boys, good boys.

Leroy and I stopped to get petrol and food on the way back to join Michael; a small family business set on land kept begrudgingly barren of sugar cane: two petrol pumps with a shop attached: hamburgers and toasted sandwiches were recommended. I paid, watching Leroy carefully as he looked around, accepting a Cherry Delight that I thought I had paid for. I was disappointed but not shocked when he smiled, and said that he had thieved it.

Both he and Mauler were the same: things were there for taking if possible, but not from everybody. They thought they had a right. I had some sympathy, because they had been buggered around so much as a race, but it was still stealing. And maybe the owner of this small business had only ever empathized with their plight . . . or maybe not.

GLADSTONE

Gladstone is a port town, an industry town, a boom town. 'The first settlers were freed convicts,' I was told by a young local with a myriad of tattoos covering most of his parched brown skin. It could have been a pretty town, but its waterfront had been prostituted to make money. A working man's town they called it. Good for business.

We camped near the horsemen and horsewomen, almost out of sideshow alley earshot. These riders followed the show route, jumping and prancing for money in each new town. After the brassy discordance of sideshow alley, sounds of impatient hooves banging against trailer walls, or the rustling of tails hunting away flies, the neighing, grunting, squealing, the sudden, playful erratic sprints of horses around makeshift enclosures left you perfectly at peace.

You heard fewer obscenities from the riders and their staff, sensed a more sober-minded community. It was a softer, slower existence, completely pleasant once you got used to the smell of horse manure.

In the early evening, Dennis lit a fire. He made it effortlessly, feeding a small flame until it grew quickly into a gale of heat, offering respite from the cool sea breeze that blew in across the harbour. Mauler was put complainingly to work scavenging more wood. Leroy and I volunteered to cook.

It is never smart to put two cooks together, even bad ones. Before long we were snapping and growling, watching each other's movements like chickens do a snake, making certain that extra ingredients were not surreptitiously added. The result was a stew of sorts, heavily flavoured with curry and strongly peppered with hot sauce. Neither of us admitted responsibility until the first words of praise were offered.

Michael and Mikey ate with us, although Mikey hardly touched his food. They left, but not before Michael brought out a carton of beer.

'Thought there was no drinking in camp?' I asked, as he laid the carton carefully on the dirt, away from the heat of the fire.

'Only when I buy, and nobody is to be invited to our fire.'

When Mauler finished his food, he laid his plate beside him in the dirt, and reached for the bong that he had made earlier out of a plastic bottle, a piece of copper pipe and foil from a cigarette packet.

'Where's the yanni, Leroy?'

'Put your dish in the washing-up basin, Mauler.'

'Aw, Leroy, you turned into an old woman or something?'

'He's right,' I said. 'We've got to start keeping the camp clean, sharing the work a bit. You might try doing something about that sleeping bag of yours, it smells like an uncleaned roo skin.'

Leroy sat calmly on a log, not saying anything, polishing his boots, which were worn and scuffed, with careful precision, nodding agreement.

'Jeez, it don't smell that bad.'

'It stinks, Mauler, just air the bloody thing,' Dennis said.

Mauler gave up, threw his bag over a clothes-line rope we had strung between the truck and a tree, and dropped back down onto his log. I passed him a beer while he sulked, head down.

Dennis said: 'Did you know Mauler is a bit of an expert on Aboriginal law? His grandfather was a king. King Cubby of the Moree mob.' When he said this Mauler raised his head, and in the glow of the firelight, his face took on a regal quality. Dennis gave me the slyest of winks.

'What about this law?' I asked.

'If say somebody ran over your kid, or killed a family member, then we go after him, it's called "payback".'

'Don't sound very Murri to me.'

'That's what we call it.'

'All right, Mauler, what do they do?'

'They spear you in the leg, and then twist it . . . or they might hit you with a nulla-nulla.'

'What if you run?'

'They get your family.'

We drank slowly, huddled around the fire, conversation spluttering, our faces flushed crimson, lines of fatigue starkly showing. Gin Gin had done us in.

'I worked a couple of years in Nicaragua. I had a fishing boat,' I answered, when Dennis asked what I had done the last few years.

'The capital's Managua, brother,' Leroy said, still examining his shoes, rubbing them now and again with a stained rag until I thought he would take the leather off.

'How did you know that, Leroy?' I asked, noticing that Mauler was slowly, vigilantly filling the bong, careful that the yanni didn't spill over into the dirt.

'What, you think we're just dumb blackfellas don't ya, Wayne?'

'No, Mauler.'

'I got a school certificate,' Leroy said with pride.

'Aw, Leroy, I'd a got a school certificate too if I'd a went to school.'

'If they didn't put you into the boys' home you mean, Mauler.'

'Leroy, you been in more jails than I have.'

'Yeah, but just for one thing.'

'Yeah, but it was a big thing. You could have killed somebody,' Mauler squealed, dragging out the word killed until it was twice as long, poking his head towards Leroy as he said it.

'What did you do?'

'Nothing, Waynee.'

'Give us some other capitals to guess.'

'All right, Leroy. Argentina,' . . . 'Buenos Aires,' 'Columbia,' . . . 'Bogota,' 'Hungary,' . . . 'Budapest.'

Nobody knew Uruguay's capital. Dennis sat silent, because foreign capitals didn't interest him, but Mauler and Leroy threw themselves into the impromptu quiz, and they were good.

I should not have been surprised. They were both impressively articulate, always reading a newspaper although they never bought one. Always discussing politics and what government decisions meant for them as Aboriginals: no reconciliation was their platform.

The first time I heard the expression, I had to ask what they were talking about, and they both shook their heads, their faces masks of disgust, before they explained to me that it had to do with the land rights issues.

'We want our country back, the country that the white man stole: all of it.'

'Do you still think we're dumb blackfellas?' Leroy asked again as we crawled onto our cots in the trailer.

'I never thought you were in the first place, I told you that. It's just that nobody I know in Australia would have a clue what the capital of Nicaragua is. I wouldn't have if I hadn't been there myself. It's got nothing to do with you being a Murri.' Leroy nodded, unsmiling, satisfied. Mauler smiled and nodded because I had given him a compliment, although I knew he really didn't care what anybody thought about him.

From my cot I caught the reflection of our fire still smouldering in a mirror that somebody had left standing on the sink. The wood had burnt down to a white powder, but red coals still flickered through the ash as if rubies had been badly hidden in a bed of fleece. The trailer was perfectly dark and my eyes closed heavily.

'The kadaicha man can get you as well.'

'What, Mauler?' I answered, bringing myself back out of the first stages of a deep sleep.

'All you have to do is give the kadaicha man a piece of cloth or a lock of hair and he's off.'

'Sounds like a bloodhound,' I mumbled, only half awake.

'He can sing you into sickness or kill you,' Mauler answered, ignoring my sarcasm.

'How do you stop him?'

'Only one way, got to have a more powerful kadaicha man.'

The next morning, Michael had us working in the same teams putting up the tent. Mauler and Leroy on the line-up board; Michael, Dennis and myself driving in the pegs and tying down the poles; all of us raising the tent. We missed the Cherbourg boys terribly.

Michael was still not satisfied. We were not fast enough, and we were still making mistakes; the angles of the pegs were not always right; the frame for the line-up board had not been put together correctly; our knots were schoolboy level; we forgot to hang out the Australian flags. We were not his pop's team of fighters.

Again, Michael was not happy with the location. We were in a far-flung corner. A good place to set up camp, but not to earn money. I foresaw trouble between Michael and Scourge.

After the tent was up, Michael told me to drive the boys downtown. Before we were even out of the showgrounds, Leroy told me he wanted to pick up his drug and alcohol addiction dole cheque.

'Let's go for a beer, Leroy,' Mauler said before we were even out of the dole office.

It was still morning and the pub was empty. When we sauntered in, the barmaid looked at us nervously, but when I ordered four beers she seemed to relax. Only Leroy noticed the change.

It was bright and cool in the pub, and the doors were flung open, letting in a breeze that was full of salt and sea. There was a pool table in the middle of the room, and a jukebox packed with cowboy music in the corner.

The barmaid poured our beers in glasses that came straight out of a fridge. In the warm air condensation formed. The glasses were wet and comforting, the beer ice cold.

Leroy put four dollars into the jukebox and we settled into a game of pool. Leroy and Mauler against me and Dennis. We were on stripes. The first song was a Buck Owens ballad called, 'Excuse Me'. A good song for a calm morning drink.

'Next town's Rockhampton, Mauler, that's Cowboy's town.'

'Oh, Dennis, shut up about Cowboy, he's gunna kill me.'

'He won't kill you,' I said, 'as long as you're not drunk and stoned when you fight him.'

'I can't fight unless I've had a drink, I told you that.' Mauler had an agitated voice, the one that came out squeaky.

Dennis sank four striped balls in a row. He laid his cue behind the white ball, lining it up with the black, rested his chin over his cue, held his head steady, and smoothly brought the cue through, striking the white ball, which struck the black neatly.

Leroy grunted as the black ball dropped into the pocket. 'I'll get beers,' and started towards the bar. 'Get a packet of smokes too, will ya, Leroy? Ours are finished.'

'I didn't care who I was fighting, Little Fella, never mattered to me, these fellas aren't real tent men,' Dennis said, as he placed the balls in the triangle ready for the next game. Mauler heard it, I could tell by the way he held the beer to his mouth, hesitating before swallowing. Dennis didn't care.

'What were you in jail for anyway, Leroy?' I asked when he returned carrying four new beers and a packet of cigarettes in his mouth.

'Tell him, Leroy,' Mauler said as he grabbed the cigarettes out of Leroy's mouth before he had even set the beers down. Leroy put another four dollars in the jukebox, waited until the music began, making sure that the right record was playing. He then sniffed deeply.

'I blew up a pub.'

'Your shot, Leroy,' Dennis said.

'The pub in Moree?' I asked.

'You heard about it?' Leroy asked, bending over the balls.

'Everybody knows about it. Not too many pubs blown up in Australia. Wouldn't let Murris in the place. Is that right?'

'Yeah, racist bastards. I was only nineteen.' And then he added quickly, 'I'd do it again tomorrow if I had to, brother. I'd blow the motherfucker to pieces all over again.' Leroy played his ball, missed the pocket badly, straightened, holding his cue by his side, and stared ahead like a soldier on parade.

'The coppers bashed the shit outa me when they caught me. I wasn't trying to get away, they just felt like bashing me.' He paused again, shuffling almost imperceptibly, remembering, because men don't forget bad bashings, the mind never lets you; I knew that.

Dennis studied the balls, Mauler did a small wild dance with his pool cue, strutting, lifting his knees high, moving in time to 'Can I Sit Next to You Girl', an AC/DC rave that had snuck in between the country. They had heard it all before.

'I got seven years and my mate got twelve because he was older and they thought it must have been his idea, but it wasn't, it was our idea. It was our political statement.'

Dennis and I left after another couple of beers, because we had to peg out the mat before the evenings fights. We drove back cautiously, conscious that we had drunk much more than the Queensland law permitted to men who drive.

When we got back to camp Michael was busy hooking up a second-hand washing machine he had just bought. It was a small, scuffed, white thing, that shook and bucked when switched on. It had one washing cycle and its timer knob was loose, but it meant we wouldn't have to go to launderettes or argue over buckets when we wanted to wash clothes.

'Where are the boys?'

'Drinking,' answered Dennis.

'Dennis, you're the camp boss, it's your job to keep them sober, I've told you that,' Michael said blinking wildly, and in a voice that sounded dispirited.

'Leroy's just got his cheque. You can't stop them boys from drinking, not when they've got money in their pockets.' Michael just nodded and turned away.

'I can't stop them, Little Fella,' he said to me in a beaten voice, before wandering to the back of the truck and pulling out the mat.

'What's up?' I asked Michael, feeling it was more than the boys drinking.

'Scourge. It's the fucking location, I'm better off paying

somebody else. Another thing, he wants twenty thousand dollars for the run, but we missed the first four towns. It's not worth it, I'm better off dealing with somebody else. Fuck, I wish I had my own ground.'

We were sitting around our fire waiting for the crowd to build up when Mauler and Leroy walked in. It was already night and they had been drinking all day; but it was hard to tell.

Dennis looked up from the potatoes he was peeling. 'Why you boys got to drink so much, wasting your money like that? Michael's giving you a chance here to make some good money, go home with something.' Michael sat on another chair, close to the fire, away from the light and said nothing.

'Aw, Dennis, we only had a few drinks.' That was all Mauler said before he asked Leroy did he have the yanni.

'It's finished,' Leroy answered as he pulled a chair up next to the fire that had burnt low.

Dennis dropped his head, shaking it slowly from side to side, letting his hair fall over his eyes and continued peeling the potatoes.

The Aboriginal who walked into our camp was sturdy. He asked permission before he moved close to our fire, but I felt if we had not given it, he would have come in anyway. He said he wanted to fight for us and to prove to us his value, he told us that he fought a number of times in Brophy's tent. He claimed to have beaten Cowboy twice.

Unasked, he picked up our axe and started to split a log that lay near the fire. He had a powerful mechanical swing, and each time the blade struck the wood that was knotted and hard, it made a deep gouge. All of us moved back.

Michael asked him to put the axe down, and he did so, but slowly and with reluctance, as if he had decided that it were his axe and his camp.

When Michael asked him if he wanted to fight that night, he declined, saying he had business, but would be back tomorrow.

'You know where we can get any yanni, brother?' Leroy asked as the man moved slowly away.

'How much did you give him, Leroy?' I asked.

'Fifty bucks. He's gunna bring us two cones later tonight.' We never saw him again.

Boom ba-boom ba-boom ! The sharp whistle, and 'Hold da, hold da.' Leroy was on the bell, Mikey stood next to me on the board, Mauler was marking out the pitch with the crowbar, rocking a little on his feet. The line undulating like a snake spoor. Two more men climbed the ladder. Showmen giving Michael a hand.

Michael took me by surprise when he matched me with a young horse handler, one of the men and women whose job it was to take care of the jumpers and prancers. 'Gee it,' he said.

Years ago I had been hit over the head with a chair in a bar fight. A brain scan showed permanent damage. Geeing it would be the only way I'd fight, but Michael knew that. The cowboy didn't know much, but he was fit and hard, and I thought we put on a good show.

Mikey boxed Scourge's boy. One throwing a lot of punches while the other covered up, and then repeated in reverse. It made for a good spectacle, and the crowd paid for it with their loose change: thirty-five dollars worth. It was a good solution, look after the young fellas.

Mauler, who Michael had decided to stop introducing as the Russian Rambo because it didn't seem to be catching on, ran out of steam and made a local port worker a hero. When the port worker's mates in their excitement and drunken state started swearing and shoving, Michael's voice boomed out of the microphone: 'No swearing or fighting, there's women and children here.'

When he said that, they settled, a deep well of decency tapped by his words and pumped to the surface. Or more likely they were just embarrassed to be singled out and then to discover that they were well outnumbered.

'We'll pay the local bloke, give the local boy a hand,' Michael said at the end of Mauler's fight. The crowd cheered. Leroy had a night off because he was too drunk.

A girl with a face that was puffy and pale as if she had never got enough sleep boxed that evening.

In the beginning, Michael argued against it. 'You'll only get hurt, darling, and I don't want to see girls hurt in my tent.' But she persisted, and Michael gave in.

With her permission, Michael put her in against a gangly factory worker when he couldn't find another girl to fight her. I thought the boy would take it easy, look after her, make it dignified, but he went all out.

He bloodied her nose with his first punch, and hurt her again a few punches later. She took it and came back. The fight went three rounds and at the end the boy was as bloodied and scuffed as the girl.

She had shown much more skill than her opponent, and her resilience and spirit were rousing, even touching, when you looked past her bloody scowl to the pretty, girlish face. She won the fight deservedly and Michael became a convert.

After the fights finished, Scourge and his wife would always walk to a quiet corner of the tent and pay the locals one by one from the night's takings. Our own fighters stood nearby in case of dissatisfaction, but Michael was always more than fair. Too fair sometimes according to Scourge, but that was only the disagreement of partners. It was during this pay ritual that Michael asked the girl to travel with us.

When she answered, moving lightly from foot to foot, I noticed she still had a line of sweat stretching across her forehead, and another above her top lip. 'I have a two-year-old daughter.'

Michael told her to bring the girl along. 'Wayne,' he said pointing to me, 'Dennis or Leroy will look after her.' He didn't mention Mauler. 'I'll think about it,' she said.

A boy with curly blond hair and the face of a cherub also fought for us that night. He was a potato cutter for a food canteen that sold only chips. Michael introduced him to the fighting public as Chippie.

Chippie boxed with a peek-a-boo style, holding his gloves high and directly in front of his young, unmarked face. And because his feet were always in the wrong position, he stumbled often. That night he gave up the potato business and joined the troupe.

'I think Chippie is gunna be another Water Boy,' Michael said to Dennis, but we could all hear it. When I asked Dennis who Water Boy was, he told me that he was a fellow who had started with the troupe as a roustabout, and had stayed for years with Michael, becoming his best fighter.

Water Boy was Michael's perfect tent man; loyal and dependable, capable. Old-fashioned qualities that his grandfather could rely on in many of his fighters.

On Michael's orders, I drove the girl home to her small apartment. 'How old are you?' I asked when I leaned over her to open the car door that was always sticking, unintentionally making her flinch.

'Seventeen,' she answered.

I had often heard showmen use the word feral when talking about their staff. To be fair, most were just honest drifters, and others just kids from bad families who couldn't stick at school, or home. But there were also outlaws, men whose names never matched any government paperwork.

On the show grounds, there were never any compromising questions asked, no references or diplomas required when applying for work. It was the French Foreign Legion for Australian misfits.

That night, a party taking place near our camp got out of hand. Show staff destroyed property on the other side of the show ground boundary fence.

The next morning when Michael found out, he took immediate action: swearing loudly, he bashed on their caravan with his fists until I thought he would put a hole in it. When they stumbled out dazed and hung-over, he put them to work cleaning up their mess and repairing the destruction. Michael then reported them to a committee of showmen whose job it was to judge on bad behaviour and set punishments.

It was a first-hand lesson on how the showmen handled problems. They didn't call in outside help, they simply marked out behavioural boundaries and policed them with vigour.

When I asked Michael what would happen, he told me that they would probably get a warning, but if it happened again they would be thrown off the grounds.

'Is that all they do?'

'If you're dealing drugs, they'll give you a hiding,' Michael said matter-of-factly.

'But everybody smokes.'

'Yeah, just don't deal in it. And respect their families or they'll get real bad. And don't go pissing around their camper trucks,' he added. And I recalled Gin Gin.

'And don't ever steal from them.'

'No plans,' I answered smiling, which brought a smile to Michael's broad face.

It was hot when we started to pack up camp. The boys were hung over and moved slowly, dodging work wherever possible. Even Dennis complained.

I thought Michael's reaction to the misbehaving show staff was a signal that he would start losing his even-temperedness with us. Most showmen I noticed had little composure when it came to dealing with their workers ineptness, and Mandy had already warned me that Michael would get harder. But he stayed patient, saw mirth in our chronic inability to learn how to put up or take down the tent, and only allowed his frustration to become noticeable during our most extreme inexpertness.

The girl came back the next day with her daughter to tell Michael she wasn't coming with us. It was the boyfriend, he didn't want her to go.

'Gee, you fought good, Little Fellow. It made me proud that I fought you. Your age, and still be able to move like that.'

'Scourge didn't think so,' I answered Dennis, lighting a cigar, concentrating on the road that was leading us inland, back into cattle country. Some of the best in the world. 'He said the fight didn't look fair dinkum. Reckoned it wasn't hard enough.'

'No, it was a good fight to watch.'

'Thanks, Leroy,' I answered, and then I heard Mauler grunt his confirmation.

ROCKHAMPTON

'Get the big ones first, and the others will back off,' Scourge said, giving me a lesson in showground survival. He then took another sip of his rum and coke and turned from me, not waiting for a reply, his attention again taken up by the pool game.

We had just arrived in Rockhampton, but because of a quirk in the show calendar, it was ten days until show time. Everybody had time on their hands and the pub was just across the road from the show grounds.

A man fell badly as he moved forward to make a pool shot, and the showmen stepped over and around him. He struggled to his feet and fell awkwardly again. When I moved forward to help, Michael held me back. He fell twice more before I understood that it was his party trick.

'He's a bull rider, he knows how to fall.' It was the showman with the movie-star looks and the fighter's nose who'd spoken to me. I recognized him as one of the drinkers from the Hole in the Wall in Bundaberg, and as one of the fighters who had backed up Michael in the Gin Gin brawl.

'Aaron,' he said, holding out his hand. 'What do you think of show life?'

Michael's patronage had assured me of not being treated roughly like many of the show staff, but besides Scourge who had been surprisingly friendly from the beginning, this man was one of the first to offer his hand.

'Tough life,' I said honestly.

'Sometimes it can be,' he answered before lifting his beer to drink, studying the game which held all our attentions over the rim of his glass. Turning to face me, he added, 'You get used to it though, you got to when you're born into it.'

He stopped talking then, rolled his back a couple of times, loosening muscles that seemed to be giving him pain, and looked around the pool room, turning his head this way and that, taking in the table, the jukebox bracketed to a far wall that blasted out rock music, and the groups yahooing men caught up in the throws of tomfoolery. Most of them young, the new generation of showmen, his tribe.

It was a confident, pleasurable gaze, one that comes from someone standing amongst his own. You see it during men's more sensitive periods: generally when they have drank not more than seven schooners, and not less than three.

A pang of jealousy tore through me! My whole life I had always felt a powerful need to move on, to leave the mob, and yet I had always been happiest when I belonged. And then the jealousy turned to melancholy, because now communities were not essential to existence, and in the future they would be less still. Soon, everybody would be a stranger.

'Your game, Aaron!' someone called out before we could speak again.

'What does he do, Michael?' I asked, as Aaron walked towards the table, taking a pool cue playfully but roughly from the loser's hand as he passed.

'Aaron, he owns the Hurricane, and Force Ten. A good bloke

93

Aaron. His grandmother drives that big pink truck. His father's got some kiddies rides on this run. His mother's on the Darwin run. That was his sister Shelly you met, the one married to the horse jumper.'

'Ron?' I asked, and Michael nodded absently.

Mauler, Leroy and Dennis were huddled around a table drinking quietly. They were the only non-showmen in that part of the pub. Fighters were accepted, as longs as they didn't put a foot wrong. Some like Dennis had gained great respect.

The bull rider fell again, and this time I thought he'd broken his shoulder, but he got up, rubbed it roughly, and fell again on the same one. Impromptu wrestling matches broke out. A glass fell and burst into a thousand pieces on the tile floor causing howls of scorn and whelps of laughter, filling the poolroom with good-natured nonsense noise. I left looking for quiet in the main bar.

'Peter Gills my name,' the drinker leaning on the bar said as he pivoted on his right elbow to face me. He was a small wiry man with a thin, deeply lined face, and his nose which was predominant, was narrow, twisted and bumpy, like it had been made from play dough by a child. A hand-rolled cigarette hung loosely from his mouth, its end stuck to his bottom lip as if it had been delicately soldered into place.

'Getting too noisy for ya in there is it, mate?' he asked as if he already knew me. 'I've seen ya with Michael.' He smiled when he said this, showing chipped, tobacco-stained teeth.

'There's a bloke in there keeps falling over,' I said, asking if he wanted a beer, and ordering two when he nodded.

'That would be my nephew.'

'Are you a bull rider too?' I asked, checking out my fellow drinkers, noting that except for Pete, I didn't recognize any as showmen.

'Usta be . . . Australian champion a long time ago when I was a young fellow. We're bull and horse breeders. You ever heard of the Gill brothers?

I nodded. 'Most people have. What are bull and horse breeders doing travelling with the show?' I asked.

'We started out as showmen. I'm the fifth generation. Jason, the one that keeps falling over, he's the sixth.'

'Started out?' I asked.

Pete stared at me, drawing his lips together, almost crushing the end of his cigarette, furrowing his forehead. Then his face relaxed and he drew on his cigarette, blowing out two lines of smoke either side of his mouth.

'We had a "wild West" tent show. It was just like Michael's, only it wasn't fighting, it was bronco busting. If you could stay on one of our horses for eight seconds, we would pay. We had whip crackers, sharpshooters, we did fancy lasso tricks.

'Mum and my aunt usta ride feature shows. Broncos,' he added when he noticed a dumb stare. 'Gee they could ride. They'd bring 'em in all right. It was mostly tent shows in the old days, families working together. You need families to run a tent show, it's labour intensive. That's what makes it hard for Michael now.'

'The showmen give him a hand,' I said.

'Yeah, that helps, but it ain't family.'

Peter paused, drew on his smoke, picked up his beer from the bar and held it tightly in his right hand, making no attempt to drink.

Dennis ambled in then, touching Pete firmly on the shoulder because they were old mates. 'You coming, Little Fella? The boys want to go.'

'Just telling Wayne about the old show days,' Pete said to Dennis.

'You're a bit older than me, Pete,' Dennis answered, dropping his head.

95

'Well, anyway,' Pete continued, sounding a little insulted, 'one time there were fifteen boxing tents going around. Country singers had their tent shows, and we had the freak shows. They weren't freaks, that was just the name they went by.'

'A lot of animal shows too. Captain Davies, Scourge's grandfather had African apes, dogs too. Them animals could do anything, ride bikes, drive go-carts, walk tightropes. Some of them apes were over five foot tall.' Pete held his hand horizontal to his chin, making sure I understood the enormity of the animal.

'Scourge's father had them too, but the animal rights people closed him down. They shut them all down,' he added, making sure I didn't misunderstand him.

'Mate, them animals had the run of the show grounds. Wouldn't have seen happier animals anywhere. Funny how some people think they know what's best.'

As he finally drank from the glass that he still held as if it were precious, I asked, 'Why was he called Captain Davies?'

'Yeah, sounds classy don't it? Just like Chief Little Wolf the wrestler. He was a Greek you know.'

'A Greek,' I repeated, remembering the name from my youth.

'It's show business, and don't you ever let him know I told you,' he added, grinning.

'Now it's only them big rides. Teenagers have all the money now and that's what they want.' Pete's head shook slowly from side to side. 'It broke families up when the tents closed down. A lot of people were forced off the show grounds. Forced us to change too. Now we've got Shetland ponies, you know, to give the kids a ride. Got a few joints too,' he added. 'We do this part of the year, and then we start supplying the rodeo circuit.'

'The boys want to go,' Dennis reminded me, and then he turned back to Pete, fingered his long hair out of his eyes, and told him how he had once knocked me out. Pete told him he already knew. 'Everybody does,' he said to me, and gave a wink, forcing a puff of smoke from the end of his cigarette.

I poked my head back through the door into the poolroom. The celebrations had drowned out the jukebox music, and the air was blue with smoke. I decided it was only a place for the showmen, waved a goodbye to Michael who seemed to be locked in earnest discussion with Scourge, and followed the boys out the door into the peace and coolness of the late night.

Next morning, I drove Mauler and Chippie to Centre-point to collect their dole cheque. Leroy, whose own money was finished, rode with us because it was Mauler's turn to pay for the revelry.

On the way back from the office, Mauler spotted a lanky Aboriginal walking along a wide footpath that skirted the road leading to downtown Rockhampton.

'Bro, where do the brothers drink?' he yelled out after I had slowed the car to match the pace of the man's walk, grunted when he got an answer, not asking the man's name, secure in his knowledge that this Murri was not from his mob. I dropped them all off at the recommended pub. Chippie drifted away in another direction.

When I arrived back at the show grounds, construction of some rides had begun, but others still lay bolted flat on their trailers, listless harlequins of steel. The joints were all locked away in the back of vans and trucks. Caravans and mobile homes were parked messily about like bleached boulders flung indiscriminately onto a bare, parched paddock.

In the Queensland winter morning heat, people were moving slowly, lost temporarily of purpose. Some wandered from camp to camp seeking out company, others busied themselves with the mending of trucks or the tending to domestic duties. A lot of the men sat around nursing hangovers. Only the children moved with a sense of direction and pace.

Later, when I returned to the pub looking for the boys, I was told by a bleary-eyed man in a slurred but assured voice, that they had gone. 'Looking for Sheila's mate.'

The Great Barrier Reef lay just off the coast. 'Islands of paradise dot crystal clear waters.' At least that's what I read in one of the glossy colour brochures at the Rockhampton tourist office I drifted into after leaving the pub. I sifted through the brochures vacantly, until the idea of having a few days away came covertly to me.

My reason for wanting to leave was not so much to see the 'islands of paradise', but rather to escape the emptiness the next days would bring.

Michael had begun to disappear more and more with his show mates, and I knew the boys would fill in their days by drinking and smoking themselves into an endless roller-coaster euphoria. It had become their habit.

I was not judging them, I just couldn't join them. I couldn't take it physically or emotionally. For me, constant alcohol obliteration brought on physical illness and depression. Smoking yanni just sent me mad.

Even knocking about with Dennis hadn't become an option, because he had also started to booze with regularity. Dennis was stricken more and more with the sadness and frustration of an old fighter whose time has passed. Travelling with the tent had exposed it and kept it persistently in his mind. To compound matters, he was also taken by a sense of purposelessness in the camp: Mauler and Leroy were not listening to him, things were going to hell, or at least not how Michael wanted them to go.

Dennis rarely mentioned his estranged father any more, and he had begun to scream in his sleep: 'Remember when I fought you, Little Fella. Gee we waz good mates in Sydney. You was my friend.

I'll knock youse all out.' It was always in the coldest, darkest part of the night, an hour before daylight that his demons found a voice. Dennis had even started talking about leaving.

Yes, I thought in that office that promised to take you to paradise, it would be good to get away for a few days. As the decision began to take hold, I even found other reasons for leaving: getting some decent, regular meals; not having to sleep on a cot like an army recruit, cook or clean; Mauler's stinking sleeping bag.

The man in the office told me there were three resorts on the island catering to young backpackers. The word resort made me cringe, but there didn't seem to be an alternative. I reserved a hut, which I later found out was only a tent, in the most normal sounding one. I returned to the show grounds to tell Michael, and that same afternoon caught a bus filled with international backpackers half my age down to the coast.

My tent was at the end of a row, and edged and shaded by non-indigenous tropical greenery, and save for the small lizards that crawled about the canvas walls hunting insects with admirable stealth and precision, it was mercifully quiet.

In the evening I drank in the resort bar alone. I had grown used to loud, physical drinking company, and it left me feeling uneasy.

I thought about joining the celebrations of my fellow islanders, but there seemed to be a bridgeless ravine between us. But why that was, I couldn't say immediately.

That night I slept so deeply that I was surprised and disorientated when I was woken by the communal, optimistic chirps and whistles of birds. I threw on a pair of swimmers and, before the sun became lethal, swam in the pristine sea, breakfasted like a starving man, covered myself with a wide-brimmed hat, bought fruit and water, made sure I had my cigars and matches, and headed out, following a trail marked on the map I had bought.

99

I arrived back just before sunset, sweaty and clear headed, prepared to spend another night drinking alone.

My reluctance to approach the backpackers had become clear to me. I had started to see them as the show-ground public: the ones who had to be mesmerized and harangued into buying tickets; the same ones who had to be psychologically and at times physically restrained when their mob instincts overtook them; as the boys and girls who sneaked under the tent flaps, scuffled, swore vilely, or screamed out for butchery during the bouts. I saw in them the local fighters who lifted knees and swung elbows with recklessness during matches, and as the ones who could make life difficult for you a hundred ways along the run if you weren't strong. Or worse, burn down your tent and take away your living: the mugs.

I was surprised how quickly I had come to distrust people. It came I knew from being part of a small tribe forever moving through other people's country.

Michael turned up the day after my walk to the other side of the island. The sun, although low, was still bright and persistent, and its reflection off the water and beach caused a glare that forced my bad eyes to squint in order to focus. When I heard my name called out, it took me seconds before I realized where it was coming from.

It was Michael's solid frame that first caught my attention, and then his heavy rolling gate on the uneven surface of the glowing sands, but until I saw his pigtail swinging from shoulder to shoulder in rhythm with his step, I wasn't certain it was him.

'Just come to see how you're getting on,' he yelled out to me, as I waded through the water to the beach.

'I'm happy to see you, mate,' I answered, meaning it like a kid whose parents arrive to take him away from a bad summer camp. 'How did you get here?'

He gave a cheeky grin this time. 'Aaron. He brought us out on his jet ski.'

'Eighteen miles?' I asked.

'Yeah, no problem, just a bit bumpy.'

'Where's Aaron?'

'Up at the bar with Jay.'

'Three blokes on one jet ski?'

'Mate, it's a big jet ski, it cost him twenty thousand dollars.'

'Mauler and Leroy are hitting the grog pretty good,' Michael told me as we walked slowly up the beach towards the Kontiki bar, a resort for thirty-five-year-olds and under.

'I knew they would. It doesn't seem to hurt them though. What about Dennis?'

'He's been with them everyday. He's getting just as bad.'

'Is he still talking about leaving?' I asked. Michael nodded, slowly.

When we arrived, Aaron and Jay had already staked out a big piece of the bar. A space had formed around them. We drank six schooners in the next hour.

This was the first time I had met Jay, who looked to be a few years younger than Aaron, and who still had that ungainly abandon that manifested itself in noise and motion of somebody who hasn't yet turned thirty. Jay wouldn't let me pay my shouts.

It could have been a generosity or something else, I thought, but either way I didn't want to accept. Australians pay their own shouts, and I couldn't afford a reputation as a bludger.

It was Michael who convinced me that it was meant sincerely. 'Mate,' he said, banging the 't', as he sometimes did when he needed undivided attention, ' showmen do it all the time, they've always got plenty of cash, that's our business, and we like to spend it.'

But I knew it was more. They wouldn't have shouted staff so easily; it was another acceptance. Michael was always lobbying for me and it seemed to be working. I hadn't asked for it, but

101

what man doesn't enjoy being part of the ruling caste. Besides, I had started to sympathize with their lot, understanding that if they were not hard, if they didn't stand solidly together, build high walls against outsiders, life could become pretty difficult. Their us against them attitude was starting to make a lot of sense to me.

We were talking about fights. Rightly or wrongly, that's what takes an important place in some men's remembered pride, and drinking with abandon always brings out prideful memories.

Michael told me about the tough man contest he fought in up in the Northern Territory a few years before. All comers, three rounds with gloves.

'Why did you fight, mate?' I asked. 'You didn't have to prove anything.'

'I needed the money,' he answered, and then he thought for a moment. 'It's what I do.'

'It's that Maori blood in you,' I said. 'Can't help yourself.'

Michael shrugged his big shoulders and blinked wildly. 'I got beaten in the final by this giant bastard,' he admitted.

Jay stared at Michael for a moment, a dumb look of disbelief on his unlined face. Then he turned to me and said, 'I heard Dennis knocked you out.' He brought his beer quickly to his mouth as soon as the words were out, pirouetted 360 degrees, taking in the other young male drinkers who had moved farther away to safety, and the curious, half-clad, sun-burned girls. Music was playing: just beats that seemed to get inside of you, and had the curious effect of making you drink faster. 'Yeah, Dennis knocked me out, but I won some too,' I warned him.

Then Aaron told a story. He was almost whispering because it was only meant for me. Michael and Jay had heard it of course, and stepped back, giving it respect, understanding that it was not meant as a boast. Aaron dropped his head at times, as if trying to bury the words in the concrete at his feet. Sometimes his voice faltered. Once he became angry.

'There was a big pub brawl and I hit this bloke. When he went down, his head hit the cement. He was dying at my feet and I didn't know.' Aaron faltered momentarily, before he said, 'It was just a fight, nobody was supposed to die.' That's when he became angry.

'I had to go to court, and I thought I would go to jail. It took two years before it was all settled. My life just stopped.' And then he said, 'But that poor bastard's still dead,' before he turned and walked towards the toilet. The boys watched him leave, saying nothing, seeming to listen to the music with no tune that still banged repetitively away.

'Mate, it's dark. How are we going to find our way back?' Michael asked nervously.

'We'll just aim for the lights,' Aaron said when he returned, his melancholy purged.

A wind had sprung up, and the sea that had been black and empty was suddenly flecked with white. The boys, dressed only in board shorts and singlets, began to rub their arms trying to sand away the cold. Michael began to shiver.

'Let's just stay here and get ourselves a hut.'

'Can't, my missus would kill me, all these young sheilas about.'

'Aaron, if we crash out there –' and Michael made a sweep with his arm, meant to represent the whole ocean '– we're dead.'

'Are you frightened, mate?' I asked. 'I didn't think you were frightened of anything.'

'But, mate, it's dangerous,' Michael answered, a silly bugger smile on his face.

'Wouldn't bother me,' I lied, which was only part lie, because I was drunk and drunks can be stupid.

'But, mate.'

'We'll leave after the next shout,' Aaron butted in, and that seemed to be the end of it.

The jet ski was parked on the beach. Aaron walked back over the sand to the bar, and asked a table of drinkers to give him a hand getting the heavy machine into the water. They ignored him, not even looking up. He gave them one more chance before screaming at them, 'Youse can all get fucked.' They looked up then but only momentarily, the insult seeming to sharpen their attentions on the beer glasses on the table in front of them.

Jay waited until they were comfortably seated on the jet ski beyond the breaking waves, before he rolled his weight to one side, tipping them into the water. He then waited until they were solidly back in the saddle, and turned it over again.

When they finally roared away, aiming vaguely in the direction of the lights eighteen miles in the distance, bumping up and down, I walked back past the table that Aaron had just insulted, aware that I was now alone, expecting problems. None of the drinkers even glanced in my direction.

I caught the boat back across the following afternoon and then another bus back to cattle country. It was still a few days until show time, but on the grounds, construction of the rides and joints had begun in earnest. A feverish, chaotic, creation of dreams was magically evolving.

I heard fierce arguments, cursing, cries of elation. Some rides were testing the volume of their music, others were running the engines of their diesel trucks, powering up their rides, filling the cleanest air in the world with poison.

Pete's Shetland ponies had escaped their tether lines and wandered calmly around the grounds like enormous long-haired dogs looking for bones. Dust, colouring the air a misty beige, caught at the back of my throat, forcing me to spit brown. It was good to be back.

The boys were not there, and when I knocked on Michael's caravan I found it locked. I was showering in the back of the trailer when Michael drove up.

'You made it back then?' I asked, pulling on a clean shirt, giving him a nod, rubbing the bristles of my hair and shaking out the water.

'Yeah,' he answered without enthusiasm, pulling at his ponytail, and looking around at the empty camp.

'We made land in twenty minutes.' He waited, then shook his head from side to side, remembering, grinning from the memory. 'Jay tipped us over again when we were out in the middle. It's the last time he's coming with me on a jet ski,' he said, his grin disappearing, turning into a playful scowl. 'I thought I might have to hook him.'

I had just asked where the boys were, when Leroy walked in. Michael frowned, but it wasn't from anger, he was a worried man. That was what was wrong with him.

'We fight in two days, you have to ease up on the drinking.'

'We will, Michael,' Leroy answered, and then he began to greet me, but was forced to turn and spit, and then to painfully dry retch as if his guts were filled with lead filings. Michael shook his head.

'I'll be right,' he assured me, before climbing the stairs into the trailer and falling on his cot like a dying man.

'Come on, let's go and get a feed,' Michael said.

'Where?' I asked, climbing into the trailer to look for shoes, and seeing the mess of boots, clothes and blankets at the back where Chippie slept. Mauler's sleeping bag didn't smell any sweeter.

'The Great Western. It's got a rodeo ring out the back of the pub, and there's one on tonight. You ever seen one?'

'Not live,' I admitted.

'They don't serve Murris in that pub,' Leroy said in a voice that was little more than a croak.

'What?' I asked, bending closer to him, making him repeat it.

'They don't serve Murris.'

'I'll find out, Leroy, and if they don't, we'll go after them.'

'Good,' he said, 'we'll blow it up.' Then I heard a catching of breath, and the beginnings of a snort that changed into a deep continuous snore.

When we drove away in the Ford, Michael was forced to lower his bull rider's hat, blocking the sharp light that streamed in from the setting sun.

In Europe, churches are built massive and central. When you wander through any town or village, you can stand in their shadows and cower. Growing up in Australia, I failed to notice that ours were built closer to the edge of town, smaller and less daunting. Or that our pubs were architecturally our most impressive buildings, or that they were the most revered. Single storey wings had been added to the Great Western's original two-storey structure so that it stretched around a corner like an earth-coloured cathedral.

We ate steaks in the main bar surrounded by a raucous, but good-natured rodeo crowd of cowboys and aficionados. Mounted bullheads decorated the walls. Unsettling, behemoth creatures, but lacking the fierce, proud gazes of the vanquished fighting bulls of Europe.

'They're all white in here,' I said to Michael, looking around the bar, suddenly remembering my promise to Leroy.

'Turn around,' he said, pointing over my shoulder with his fork that still had a piece of almost raw meat impaled on its tongs.

Three Aboriginals, heavy, dark men, were sitting on high stools in the next room doing something that I couldn't make out.

'They're playing the pokies,' Michael said, guessing my question.

'Good,' I answered, 'saves blowing up the place.'

'He wasn't kidding you know,' Michael reminded me, gnawing on his bone because the red gristly meat that was left was too scant to cut with a knife. 'At least I don't think so.'

'What's worrying you?' I asked, feeling things were not right.

'Nothing,' he answered sharply, and then he walked to the bar, returning with two new beers.

'I'm broke,' Michael suddenly admitted when he sat down again. 'If we don't make some money here, I might have to give up.'

'I didn't know it was that bad.' I said it sincerely, sadly, because if Michael failed, it was the finish of all of us. 'I know the crowds haven't been that big, but I still thought you were ahead.'

'Mate,' he started, giving me a patient look, 'I'm paying the boys four hundred dollars a week, there's the ground to pay for, Scourge, you, diesel for the truck, petrol for the car, the food, and we've been sitting on our arses for over a week. I haven't sent any money home for ages. Mandy's got nothing, she's even baking bread for the kids to take to school. And Brophy is going to be in Rockhampton, and we're not going to make anything again.' I wanted to pay for the meal, but Michael wouldn't hear of it.

The Great Western had added a big shed to the back of the pub. Just a roof supported by steel girders, but it was vast. A circle of steel fence shaped the dusty rodeo arena. A setting for a spectacle.

The whelps, whistles, screams and timorous gasps from the crowd watching the rodeo drew us outside. It was cold, almost bitter after the warm day, and we both moved without consultation towards one of the fires burning in the drums that been placed around the area.

'I'll get us some drinks,' Michael said, moving towards the outside bar.

'Rum!' I yelled after him. He nodded, understanding, not looking back. Men in large hats crowding the area made way for him.

I heard the bang of a heavy gate being thrown open, and a dirty-coloured bull, a horned, twitching mass of muscle, came heaving and twisting out of the chute. His rider lost his hat almost immediately, but with one hand wrapped into the bull rope, and the other flaying loosely in the air as if it had pulled from its socket, he hung on like a shaken rag doll.

He was finally thrown by an unexpected, explosive jackknife, landing with a dusty uncoordinated thud on his backside. The rider rolled immediately to his feet and, while two rodeo clowns occupied the bulls attention, rushed to retrieve his hat. Only later, when the bull stood in the middle of the empty arena looking despairingly around for something else to charge, could two mounted horsemen goad him back into the pens.

'They didn't want to serve me because I'm black,' Michael said, returning with two rum and Cokes.

'You're not black,' I said, surprised that he thought he was. 'Did they say something?'

'No, just took their time serving me, and there's nothing wrong with being black.'

'I never said there was. I only said you weren't.'

'That's not what a lot of people think in Australia. I get that shit all the time . . . you'll notice.'

'It's most likely because you look like a bad bastard. You're big, and that plait; you probably frightened them.'

'No, it's because I'm not white. Sometimes you forget that I'm Maori. You know I reckon Leroy's right, they don't like Murris here.'

We watched a few more riders strap themselves to the backs of terrifying bulls in heroic, suicidal efforts to remain mounted for eight seconds, and then it was finished.

'I'll get a couple of drinks. What's next?'

'The saddle broncs,' Michael answered distractedly, while turning to glance at two passing cowgirls, both wearing star-and-stripe-patterned shirts and jeans that stretched so tightly around every curve and over every swelling that it made you suspect they were painted on. Both smiled when they noticed they were being appreciated. One tipped her hat in acknowledgement.

'Seems to me women like black men,' I said when I returned with the drinks.

'Handsome black men,' Michael answered.

A roar from the crowd that had become larger and more vocal was the first warning that the rider was coming out of the chute.

I found the bulls a powerful, mindless movement of violence. You had to admire them, but wonder why anyone would dare ride one. The horses were different; I didn't sense any hateful or deadly purpose; I found their twisting, bucking and pirouetting eurhythmic; I admired their great leaps, their balance and deliberation.

'Why don't you like Brophy?' I asked, after watching more cowboys being flung dismissively to the ground. Only one stayed the eight seconds, and was lifted off the still bucking horse by a pick-up rider who wrapped an arm around his waist as if they were sweethearts.

'I told you, he's not a member of the showman's guild, and he tells everybody his boxing tent has been around for generations. It hasn't.'

I thought it was something more. Michael had not toured with Bell's for eight years, and during that time, Brophy's name had unfairly become synonymous with tent fighting. Michael's grandfather had started his tent eighty years ago, and now all people talked about was Fred Brophy. I'd be mad too.

A band had just started to play the sweet sentimental sounds that cowboys like to drink to when Michael told me it was time to leave. He had invited me to the showmen's picnic the next day, and it started early.

When I stepped out of the caravan dressed to run the next morning only Dennis was up and about. He nodded at me in that quiet way he had of acknowledging you. 'Making coffee, Little Fella, do you want some?'

'Yeah,' I answered, 'I'm too crook to run anyway. I'll put on some toast.' As Dennis fiddled around with the jug, trying to find a plug that worked by the light of a single forty-watt bulb, I asked him about his father.

'I saw him,' he said, but didn't elaborate. I thought then that he didn't find what he was looking for. It had been a lifetime since they had seen each other, two rushing rivers of time welling up against one another: the big old German with the clear blue eyes, and the middle-aged Aboriginal tent fighter he had not seen since childhood.

'I think I'm gunna go home, Little Fella. I don't want to let Michael down, but the boys don't need me, I'm not doing any good here. Michael's paying me for nothing.'

'Michael does need you,' I told him sincerely.

We let it rest then, sipping our coffee, warming our hands on the mugs, nibbling our toast wordlessly. The sun was rising, glowing like a small distant scrub fire, subtly heating everything it shone on. The sad, murky-morning light became sharper, our voices louder, the content of our conversation more optimistic. All of a sudden, we found ourselves sitting under a clear blue sky full of fight. I told Dennis about my walk over the island and he listened enthusiastically, because he understood the need to wander off sometimes.

*

110

Michael, Mikey and myself drove off to the showmen's picnic before the other boys had rolled out of bed. Dennis didn't mention leaving to Michael. All Michael said to Dennis was that we would put the tent up tomorrow.

The picnic that was always celebrated on the same day at the same place, was held at a public park, next to a beach on the coast; one meant for families. There were benches scattered about a large tree-shaded area, and the local parks authority had built a shed in case of rain.

Each family brought food and drink that they spread about and shared like a May Day feast in Moscow. Games and competitions were organized, and prizes were given out. Michael and Mikey as men alone were taken care of by whatever group they chose to stand amongst. Some wondered what I was doing there, but I was made welcome.

The showmen could have been bus drivers at their yearly picnic. In their extraordinary life, the ordinariness of the day confused me. Michael told me he thought it was a good way of getting to know people, and then he asked me to manage him next year.

When we got back to camp, we heard that Brophy and Cowboy Wilson had arrived. Scourge called us from the pub claiming that they were running down Bell's.

'You don't have to come with me,' Michael said when I warned him that looking for trouble was not going to help anything.

'I don't look for trouble,' he added, an angry look coming to his face.

'I'm coming,' I said.

When we arrived, Cowboy Wilson and Brophy were sitting at a table in the main bar with Peter Gill and Scourge. Brophy leaned heavily on the tabletop, both hands clutching a whisky glass. He was so deep in conversation with Pete, that he didn't even notice us sitting down.

I concentrated on Cowboy Wilson who looked liked he was also drinking whisky, but unlike Brophy, was sipping his slowly. I had heard so much about him, but nobody I had spoken to had actually seen him. He had become a legend in our camp through hearsay.

He was smaller than I had expected. He wore a white cowboy hat and a narrow-cut, black jacket embroidered on the shoulders. He reminded me of a television cowboy, but I couldn't think who.

I was confused because the atmosphere was civil and I hadn't expected that after Scourge's telephone call. Even Scourge was making polite conversation.

'I heard you were Australian champion?' I asked, when I got the chance. 'I'm with Bell's,' I said as a way of introduction.

'I was,' he confirmed, speaking modestly, concisely, surprising me, because words were not normally a fighter's best expression of intelligence.

I could hear Brophy talking over Cowboy Wilson's story, and I looked sideways at him. He looked Pete's age and his face, although weathered and red, was still handsome. His most startling feature I thought was his impressive head of grey hair. I noticed that he was going to fat.

I listened only a few moments before I recognized Brophy as blusterer, someone who thrives on attention. After Michael sat down his voice tapered off, his stories broke up. He knew Michael had the same ones and better. They left shortly after we arrived.

'I liked him,' Scourge said, coming back from the bar with new drinks all round.

'Cowboy,' I said. 'Yeah, I liked him too.'

'Roy Rogers,' I suddenly said to nobody.

'What?' asked Scourge.

'That's who he reminded me of.'

It took us all morning to put up the tent. Rope pegs and poles were missing, only to be found again in the most unexpected places. Mauler and Leroy forgot how to put together the frames that held the line-up board. Banners were hung upside down.

When Dennis and I finished laying down the mat, it was full of hollows and bumps and so loose that it resembled an unmade bed. We took turns banging in the pegs, unable to swing the heavy hammers and breathe for any length of time.

Sweat poured across us like downpour run-offs. Leroy dry retched continuously. When we ran in the king poles in the heat of the day, it was a great relief to see the tent lift and stand to be counted amongst the attractions of dreams.

'That was bloody terrible,' Michael told us after we had finished.

'Aw, Michael,' Mauler began, but Michael cut him short.

'You've been on the piss for over a week, Mauler, now you can't even put up the fuck'n' tent.'

'Was I all right, Michael?'

'No, Chippie, you were missing half the time, and I don't want to see any more girls coming around here while we're working. Do you understand?'

Chippie nodded, looking directly at the ground, his blond curls falling over his face. 'All right, Michael.'

'Keep off the piss, we've got to fight tonight,' was his last order, and then he left.

The boys and Dennis walked away together, drifting off through the small family crowd that was wandering mesmerized along sideshow alley. Mauler walked with his arms hanging down by his sides, glaring from side to side, frightening people unintentionally.

Chippie looked like a scuffling albino between Dennis and Leroy. I noticed that he never lifted his feet.

Dennis stopped before they were out of earshot. 'You coming?'

'Where?'

'To get a drink.' I shook my head and Dennis nodded.

'You'll have to fight Cowboy tonight,' I heard Dennis say to Mauler before they started to move off again. Mauler strode angrily away, not answering or looking back.

The noise was already deafening, the air stank of diesel, but the spruikers had nothing to do. The rides weren't turning, and when I looked up at the Ferris wheel, its gondolas were empty. The first hours of the show were always like an outlandish, extravagant party without guests.

Later I went looking for Brophy's tent. I wandered along the dusty alleys, stopping to talk to some of the joint operators, declining free rides on Aaron's Hurricane and the Big Whizzer, finally passing a food stall advertising barbecue beef rolls. Michael called out to me from behind the canteen.

'Where are you off to?'

'I'm going to have a look for Brophy's'

'Come and get something to eat. Where are the boys?' he asked.

'Don't know,' I lied, 'but I think Chippie is taking some rides, or he might be out with his girls.'

'The girls like him all right,' Michael said as he handed me a big bread roll filled with blood-rare slices of beef.

'Who owns this place?'

'One of my mates.' And then a neat, clean-cut man in his thirties came out of the canteen and joined us. Michael introduced him as Darren.

'You want something to eat, just come here. If I'm not here, tell them I sent you, and you won't have to pay,' he said to me after shaking my hand, and then he went back to serve another customer.

'Thanks,' I mumbled, happy with the change of diet.

We ate the sandwiches sitting in the aromatic shade of a big old eucalyptus, on grass that had been recently cut.

'Darren is a third generation showman,' Michael told me. 'His father's got the kiddie rides and the Mousko circus. You know, the tent with mice running over see-saws and up ladders?' When I confirmed with a nod that I knew, he continued, 'They die on him all the time.'

'What?' I asked, barely able to pronounce the word around a mouth full of bread and meat.

'The mice, they keep dying. People come to look at them and there are corpses everywhere.'

Darren was uncharacteristically soft spoken for a showman. Not showground tough, at least not appearing so. He was one of the last generation of showmen not to be educated by the travelling schools. He couldn't read or write, but only because he didn't care to learn. Michael told me that he owned nineteen food canteens. Darren was a millionaire.

I left when Michael's phone rang. It was Michael's mother. I knew because Michael's voice softened almost to a coo when he answered.

I have never embraced the new culture of carrying telephones because I am fearful of being so contactable. When I was younger, I sometimes travelled years without writing or calling loved ones. I was always afraid of news because it could be bad. No news was better. I have never lost that fear. A consequence of this dread is that I am able to shut out one life, and become wholly part of another.

Overhearing part of Michael's conversation with his mother as I walked slowly away made me realize that I had yet again deserted another life. It was as if my business in Estonia didn't exist, or that the brown languid canal that flows in front of my Amsterdam apartment drifted in front of somebody else's.

115

I'd forgotten that my cupboard was full of heavy winter clothes, and that I'd left my bicycle chained to a bridge that lifted like a rearing stallion when canal boats passed under. I'd put out of my mind the rattling keys that opened the interminable locks of my world, and the multitude of bills that needed to be paid as a price for a European city life.

I tried not to think about my wife of twenty years, or my half of the soft bed that I shared with her. About the good wines we drank most nights with the food that she cooked with care. About theatres, restaurants, the national ballet that performed at the end of my street, or morning coffee in warm dark bars that reeked of stale cigarette smoke and conviviality. About sunny winter terraces. But this time I had extra reason for forgetting: if I didn't, I would become weaker, and on the show grounds you can't afford to be weak.

Brophy's tent was an ochre colour. If you erected it in the Simpson Desert, you could easily mistake it for a rock outcropping. They had put it up next to a tall pine near the main entrance gate. It was the best spot.

A likeness of Fred Brophy had been painted in the middle of the tent banner. Cowboy Wilson, wearing boxing trunks and his signature white hat, hands held ready to fight, stood next to him. There were likenesses of other fighters from a bygone era: the fighting Moore Brothers, the sons of Selby Moore, the original owner of the tent, the man Brophy claimed family to; and Tony Mundine, our esteemed Aboriginal champion, Dennis's old sparring partner and mate. There were others.

When Brophy finally climbed onto the line-up board wearing a startling fuchsia-coloured shirt, long shadows were shading most of the tent, making the shirt appear murky and unremarkable. It was only when he moved into the sunshine that still reached part of the board that the shirt sparkled like a pink-tinted mirror. I thought it was too early in the day, but as soon as he started his patter, a crowd gathered.

He brought up a fighter to start banging the drum and another to ring the bell, and the crowd began to assemble in earnest. Boom ba boom ba boom . . . It was the same beat, the tent fighter's beat. He lined up his boxers who were impressively draped in emperor-yellow satin gowns. Strangely, they were all white. Cowboy Wilson stood in the middle of the board.

On an unseen signal, the drummer ceased his banging and Brophy started to match his fighters with men in the crowd.

I thought I should be getting back, but his patter kept me glued. It wasn't as historically underpinned or as dramatic as Michael's, but he had a tale that could keep you lingering. Brophy used different words, but they carried the same message: step up and make a man of yourself. Show the world, or yourself what you're made of.

You would think that an experienced life would help you see through such a challenge, understand it for what and who it was meant; it had nothing to do with aging, mediocre ex-pugs. Certainly not for ones with brain damage.

Suddenly and irrationally, I wanted to fight one of Brophy's men. I began picking out the fighters on the board who looked my weight, and each moment I stood there listening to Brophy, and not taking up his challenge, I felt as worthless as I knew Dennis felt. It must be an old fighter's or old fool's affliction.

I didn't put up my hand. Fear for my damaged brain kicked in, but I also I knew I would have been recognized as a Bell's worker, and what would Michael say. Especially if I lost badly.

There were no side walls to Brophy's tent. Bales of hay had been placed around the mat, which gave an ordered, ascetic impression, but had the effect of tripping up the fighters when they were forced back onto them, and keeping the public at bay.

117

In Bell's tent, the public sat around the edges of the ring. They were the hay bales. There was the danger of crushing them, or of accidentally involving them in a melee because of an errant swing or because a combatant was punched or forced into a group of the worst sort of mugs, but that was part of the excitement and the paying customer deserved that. Brophy's tent was full, the consequence of gratis entry.

Cowboy Wilson stood calmly in his corner, still wearing his white hat as his seconds pulled firm new gloves onto his outstretched hands. I noticed he was wearing hand wraps and boxing boots, and that he was well trained.

Fred Brophy, standing in the middle of the hay bale ring, the synthetic light making his greying hair dull and his fuchsia shirt dazzle, introduced him as the undefeated tent-fighting champion. It was an unusual fight because two men were presented as his opponents and there were two referees.

Wilson moved elegantly around the first, a taller, heavier boy, easily slipping his swings and punches, which were youthfully fast and potentially ruinous, countering with sweet, copybook left hooks and at times straight rights that were delightfully timed and, when landing, sounded not unlike a tennis ball being struck by the middle of a tightly strung racket.

We didn't have anyone like Cowboy Wilson. He fought like a professional boxer. He had elegance and discipline, but it was out of place.

The fights were only three rounds, and his countering style left gaps, moments of emptiness, and to make up for that he chose to showboat. Take risks.

He was a fighter, but I didn't think his textbook style would allow him to last as long as Michael had in the tents. Hands up, push your opponent back, force him to work, and then hook the body and head. That's how Michael had explained it, and he had me convinced. Cowboy Wilson couldn't stand up to Michael or Mauler, not in a tent, not if we took away those bales and one of those referees.

When Wilson boxed the next man who was much smaller than the first, and with almost no fighting skills, he played with him. Not like a cat does with a mouse, I didn't detect any cruelty, only concern to keep the fight going for the public and not to hurt the man too much. Then Cowboy faced the tall boy again, and when trying to put together a combination, ran into a left hook that left him unconscious on the mat.

Brophy dragged him back to the corner and replaced him with a hulk of man who wrestled the tall boy around the ring until Cowboy Wilson recovered. When Wilson came back out, he boxed more cautiously, hands held higher, waiting instead of taking the fight to the boy. His chance came, and it was also a left hook that put the tall boy out.

It wasn't right, the tall boy had been worn down by the hulking man and robbed of his victory. I felt sorry for him because he deserved his glory, but I also felt sorry for Cowboy Wilson.

Maybe Wilson needed the money, but I think he kept fighting for the roar of the crowd. Most fighters do.

He had told me in the pub that he had suffered eight knockouts in a row. Through experience, I knew your reactions slow, your sight misleads you and your brain closes down more easily after a couple of knockouts. Wilson wouldn't have been knocked down by this boy in his professional days, he would have seen them coming. And if a punch had got through, he would have taken it standing.

I watched a few more of Brophy's boxers and walked out knowing that I could have beaten any of them near my weight.

I found the boys in a show-ground bar. Horses and cattle were penned in the sheds and yards behind the building. At times you could hear the desperate, confused bellowing of the cattle, or a squeal from a horse after suffering a bite or kick from a stablemate, but you had to listen carefully, because the noise made by the drunken men in the bar was not insubstantial.

Heavily tattooed women with badly bleached hair shuffled amongst these men, not seeming to belong to any group. But that was deceiving.

The boys were drinking with another Aboriginal. A stocky man who smiled often. He wore a black T-shirt with 'Who's Your Daddy?' written on the chest, a gold neck chain, and a black pork-pie hat set at a carefree angle. He looked like an old-fashioned crooner, somebody who would sing into a woman's eyes. A ladies' man.

'This is Bundy,' Dennis said to me as I sat down.

'Wayne, you gunna buy us a beer? You haven't bought any in a week.' I shook Bundy's hand, before giving Mauler money to buy five cans of beer. He was drunk, they all were.

'Why do you keep buying him beers, Little Fella?'

'I bought you a beer too, Dennis,' I replied, and then I asked him, 'Is something wrong between you and Mauler?' Dennis dropped his head, not answering.

'What's going on, Leroy?' I asked when he returned to our table. He had been talking to one of the tattooed women, calling her sister, touching her shoulder, using her to balance.

'Dennis has been putting the wind up Mauler all day, telling him Cowboy's gunna give him a hiding.' Leroy slurred a little, his balance went again, but this time he used a chair to remain upright. 'And Mauler and Dennis had a fight in Moree.'

'What, when?' I asked, surprised no one had told me.

'A while back . . . out the back of the pub.'

'Who won?'

'Mauler beat him bad, but Dennis wouldn't give up. Mauler had to walk away in the end because Dennis still wanted to fight him.' Leroy sipped from the can I had just bought him and wandered unsteadily back to the woman he called sister.

A terrible shame for a man like Dennis, even to be beaten by someone fifteen years younger and as good as Mauler. Fighting had been Dennis's life, he was known as a fighter and fighters are supposed to win. For everybody, but mostly for yourself.

I caught Dennis moving cautiously towards Mauler out of the corner of my eye. I had no doubt that he was lining him up for a king hit. I moved in between them. Dennis gave up then, his shoulders dropped, his fists unclenched. I had hindered his moment of madness.

'Come on, we've got to fight tonight,' I said to them. 'Mauler, go and get Leroy before we have to fight for him.'

'Come on, Leroy,' Mauler yelled out, 'she don't want nobody as ugly as you.'

We started back through the crowd that had grown steadily since the afternoon, forcing us to weave and lightly jostle to make headway. But it was still a family crowd, not our crowd, and I wasn't looking forward to Michael's welcome.

He was testing the sound system when we returned. It was easy to see that the boys had been drinking heavily and I expected a lecture, but he seemed light hearted, relaxed, and said nothing.

'Are we going to fight Brophy's men, Michael?' Mauler asked him immediately.

I had never understood Mauler's fear of Cowboy. His reputation had been built up to mythic proportions, but nobody was that good, and I had never seen Mauler troubled by another fighter. His fear was irrational, and I suspected the drink was starting to play his nerves.

'No,' Michael said, 'we'll fight here tonight.'

When Michael said this, Mauler's shoulders straightened. 'Come on, Leroy, let's get ready.'

'I've got money,' Michael said to me after they left, reaching up at the same time to tighten one of the speakers.

'How?' I asked.

'I sold the extra tent to Darren's dad.'

'You've got another tent?'

'You think I tell you everything?' Michael answered, grinning mischievously, before continuing. 'He's got some of the money.'

'Why not the lot?' I asked, wondering vaguely where the tent had been stored.

'That's the way we do it on the show grounds. When cash comes in, things get paid, and they always get paid.'

'Good,' I said. 'I saw Cowboy fight.'

Michael continued fiddling with the speakers, completely disinterested. But that was only an act.

'You and Mauler would both beat him,' I said. 'You're both too strong and you hit too hard. There's not enough room in the ring for him to get away from your big punches.' And then I added, 'He's a beautiful boxer though.'

When Michael turned to face me he was smiling. 'Crowds'll get bigger the further up we travel.' And then he said, 'Both of us you reckon?' I nodded, knowing then that Michael had lost interest in taking on Brophy. What would be the point?

Boom ba boom ba boom . . . Leroy was on the drum. 'We travel the length and breadth of Australia . . . Any of you local blokes out there thinks he can fight?'

'Wayne, where's Dennis?' Michael called urgently down to me, as I busied myself finding gowns for the fighters.

'Still at the pub, I suppose.'

Michael shook his head. A disappointed shake, not an angry one. 'You take the ladder, Wayne, and don't let anybody up it until I tell you. Get Chippie up here, and tell Mauler to be ready.'

Scourge and Leanne were already on the door. I nodded as I passed them, noticing absently that they both held a roll of tickets. Outside, the coloured lights hurtling willy-nilly through the dark night mesmerized me momentarily. I could hear Chippie ringing the bell; a disjointed clang with no seeming federation to the beat of the drum.

'What's the tickets for?' I asked Scourge, turning to face him, giving myself a moment's respite from the work ahead.

'Michael wants to know how many customers we're getting, and he wants us to write down the names of the local fighter and what we pay them. It's a waste of time, cash is faster . . . a waste of time,' Scourge repeated. I nodded but said nothing, it wasn't my affair how they did business together.

Dennis turned up a little later with Bundy, but didn't offer to take the ladder, preferring to stand amongst the crowd. Bundy agreed to fight for Michael.

After Mauler marked the pitch with his crowbar, scowled and threw a few threatening punches, Michael called for the drum and bell. He studied the crowd momentarily, and then we heard his sharp whistle and 'Hold da, hold da.' Chippie, I noticed, was already keeping better tune.

Bundy was matched with a man who I had seen fighting a gee in Brophy's tent, but this wasn't a gee and, after hours of passive drinking with Dennis, Bundy was relishing the movement. Crouching, swaying, throwing left hooks as if he was scything wheat. At times as referee, I had to cajole his opponent into fighting harder. Brophy's man flopped down on his stool at the end of the second round and refused to come out for the third.

Chippie fought a pale, tall, narrow boy with bad teeth, who Michael had named Skinhead, because of his shaved skull. He was light punching, unbalanced and uncoordinated, but against Chippie's shuffling, stiff attack, it was an even fight. Leroy, breathing awkwardly, survived another three-rounder. There was no one big or game enough to take on Mauler.

The other fights were between the locals. Michael had an extraordinary knack of matching boys that would produce brutal, blood-letting affairs. But he would never let them get out of hand. He watched every fight closely, constantly instructing me from behind the side wall to part them, check for cuts, exhaustion, desire to continue. As referee, I was like a puppet on his string.

After the fights, Scourge paid off the local fighters one by one, before taking the gate money for safe keeping to his mobile home. He returned with cans of rum and Coke for Michael and myself. Because of his rough reputation, even, or especially amongst most of his fellow showmen, I was always taken aback by his friendliness to me. It wasn't mercenary, I couldn't do anything for him. I suspected he had a sweet side that he couldn't do anything about.

As we left to drink in the Hole in the Wall, I noticed Leroy by the side of the tent. It was too dark to see properly, but by the sounds he was making his dry retching had developed into full-fledged vomit. Better for the guts, I thought.

'How did we do?' I asked Michael, after buying three more rums.

'Ask Scourge, he's got the money,' Michael answered a little sharply.

'We'll cover costs if we get a few more good houses,' Scourge answered, not noticing, or taking notice of Michael's insinuation. 'We'll do better once we get up further north to the little places.

These big towns are no good for us, too much competition. They're spoilt for entertainment around here.'

We left after Michael's shout. I was ready, I needed the sleep, and I still wasn't comfortable drinking in the Hole. It was the club for the hard core showmen, and I reckoned I'd never make membership.

Dennis screamed again in the night. 'I'll knock youse all out. Gee you was a good bloke. I usta spar with you, Tony. I'll kill youse all, I'll kill youse,' and then it became just a scream.

I had just got back from my run as Dennis climbed slowly down from the trailer. It was already light, and I had never known him to get up so late.

'I'll make the coffee today,' I said to him.

He nodded, holding his head with both hands, flopping into a stool before using his fingers to scratch through his hair. When I gave him his cup he mumbled a thanks, but almost so quietly that I couldn't hear it. 'I'm leaving, Little Fella, I'm not doing any good here.'

'When?' I asked.

'As soon as I can get a bus back south.'

Dennis told Michael when he came out of his caravan. 'All right, Dennis, I'll take you into town later. You got some more coffee, Wayne?' And then he drank it walking away.

Dennis disappeared after breakfast and when he returned, he showed me a pocket full of complimentary tickets for rides he had collected from the showmen.

'My family might visit today, and I want them to have a good time,' he said to me when I asked about the tickets. 'I hope they come before Michael wants to leave.'

They did come. One boy, a handsome teenager, almost as light as Dennis, was introduced to me as his son. I remembered vaguely between conversations about Dennis's father that there had been mention of a son born from an affair with a boss's daughter, a white woman.

It was one of those relationships that liberals think should blossom, but in reality has very little chance. Especially all that time ago, in a state renowned for poor racial harmony and social inequalities. Dennis had told it in passing and, I felt, with some feelings of remorse.

I couldn't remember whether Dennis had ever seen the boy, only that when the affair finished, he had no idea she was pregnant. There were other children and adults in the group that visited Dennis that day, and I thought that there might be a connection with his father, but who they were remained a mystery.

Peace is subjective. A professional soldier, a friend of mine, once told me that he had never felt calm since his second tour of duty in Vietnam had finished more than thirty years before. 'I knew what I was doing over there, and I couldn't know it better . . . that's peace.' I hadn't yet met a showman who was happier away from the noises, smells, movement and tensions of the show-ground.

My peace came from sitting alone in the grandstand, shaded from the sun, separated from the sideshow alley, gazing out over the show-ring at the jumpers who leapt and lifted, carrying their riders over impossibly high fences.

If I looked towards the sideshows from such a distance, the rides flew and fell in slow motion, the strong bleaching light of day faded the colours, the music was only a background tangle of notes and unfathomable words that you could allow in or shut out, the dust, a musty-coloured vapour 'over there', the smells non- existent, the crowds a swirling, isolated sea of far off movement. I needed this peace every now and then, but only for short stretches of time, and this need was becoming less and less the further we travelled.

When I got back to camp, Mauler was washing the hill of dirty dishes. The cots and clothes chests had been carried outside, and a small cloud of dust wept from the trailer. When I looked inside, I saw a thin, pale, white girl with short, straight brown hair sweeping dirt towards me. 'My name's Kassi, I'm with Fuggsi,' she said, smiling sweetly. Ash fell intermittently from a cigarette that hung from her mouth.

I heard loud talking inside the tent, and when I looked inside I saw Leroy and a stranger, another Aboriginal, picking up the rubbish left by the mugs the night before. They had already swept the mat, filled the water bottles, hung up the towels used to soak up blood and sweat, and placed the lockers containing the gloves and gowns ready for the night's fights. The place had never looked better.

'Good job,' I said.

'Waynee, this here is Fuggsi,' Leroy said standing with an empty cigarette packet in one hand and a sweet wrapper in the other, gesturing towards the stranger with the sweet wrapper. Fuggsi was shirtless, and a light sweat covered his hairless chest. He wasn't big, at least he didn't seem big enough for his reputation. The boys had described him as one of the hardest men to come out of Moree.

I nodded to Fuggsi, smiling at the same time. He came over and gave me his hand. It was a firm shake, too firm, and he pumped it a little too much. He was testing me.

'Got to keep them boys working, Wayne, they're lazy, man, all they want to do is drink and smoke.' He spoke with a heavy nasal influence as if his nose had been broken, but when I looked, I saw only one that was narrow and patrician. When I looked a little more closely, I detected a slight spread high up on its ridge, and then I saw the break.

'I'm not the boss,' I replied.

'You're the white fella, aren't ya? White fellas are always the boss.'

'Not this time,' I answered.

When Chippie came in, Fuggsi said, 'Hey man, you gunna give us a hand?'

'Give Mauler a hand finishing the dishes, will you, Chippie?' I asked, and Chippie picked up a tea towel and began wiping.

'See, I told ya, man . . .'

'Me and Mauler told him you were a good bloke, a fair dinkum white bloke,' Leroy said to me after the work was done and Fuggsi had left with his girlfriend to have a look around the show.

'Thanks,' I answered, 'I think he's trying to find out for himself.' And then I went looking for Fuggsi. 'We all right?' I asked, when I found him by the shooting gallery.

'Yeah, man,' he said to me, knowing what I meant. 'Me and you don't have any problems.' And after that we never did.

'What do you think of Fuggsi?' Michael asked me when he saw the clean camp.

'He's got a lot of energy, seems to be able to get the boys moving, got a nice car. I like him,' I said.

'Yeah,' Michael answered thoughtfully, 'he's a bit different to the rest of the boys. I'm thinking of making him camp boss now that Dennis is leaving.'

Dennis moved out with little fuss. After his family left he quickly packed his bag and waited patiently for Michael. I made us a couple of coffees and sat with him in the shade of the tent. He was quiet, something was on his mind, but it was always hard to tell what with Dennis. 'I hope you don't think bad of me,' he suddenly said, and then he went quiet again.

'Michael's gunna miss you,' I answered. 'Me too,' I added seriously, sadly.

The boys had all left and we were completely alone. The tent protecting us from the crowds that flowed through sideshow alley like a benevolent invading army.

'You know when we fought, Little Fella?'

'Yeah,' I answered, expecting another version of the knockout.

Dennis hesitated until I thought he was not going to say anything. 'You had me beat, Little Fella.' Then he smiled and nodded at me.

I could recall the punches as if I were still throwing them. How I ducked and weaved, easily avoiding Dennis's punches, catching him repeatedly with solid rips and hooks. I remembered as clearly as if it were today, because I had never thrown them more sweetly.

And then the memory of climbing slowly up from the canvas, unsure of how it happened. Standing, shaping up, driving Dennis momentarily backwards, and then climbing off the canvas again. And finally standing helpless with my guard down, while Dennis pounded away with head shots until the ref saved me from myself.

'I went back to my corner and told my trainer that I couldn't hit you. If I didn't land that right hand, you would have beaten me, Little Fella.'

I had thirty years to think about that fight because it had been my first loss, and it had been the harbinger to my boxing future. Thirty years to realize that I might have bamboozled Dennis for a couple of rounds, but I could never have beaten him, he had too much fight.

Dennis belonged to the hunters of the ring, and I was more like the clever prey. I could always give them a good run, but in the end they'd corner me. Still, it was nice of Dennis to say that.

*

The sound of a car horn dragged both our minds back to the present. We stood and walked into the sun. Dennis handed me his empty coffee cup, shook my hand and got in beside Michael, throwing his bag onto the back seat. The big black car that looked more dented than ever because Fuggsi and the boys had washed it crawled past the showmen's camper vans towards the exit gates, careful of the children who had just gotten home from their travelling show-school.

After the sun disappeared, it cooled quickly, and when Mauler and Leroy got back from the bar, they made a fire in an old cut-down oil drum. Bundy, the ladies' man, and another Aboriginal returned with them. Both wanted to fight in the tent that night. Michael gave the new man the nom de guerre 'Black Snake'.

'Where you been, Fuggsi?' Mauler asked, accepting the bong from Leroy, drawing deeply, spluttering lightly, before handing it to Black Snake, as Fuggsi and Kassi walked out of the dark, and into the firelight.

'I had to collect some money, man. He didn't want to pay me the cunt, but he did in the end.' Fuggsi moved from foot to foot, his eyes darted to each man standing around the fire. 'I knocked the fuck'n' cunt right off the veranda.'

In Queensland, the houses are built on posts to keep them cool, and to keep out the vermin. It's a long way from veranda to ground.

Kassi stood close to him, at times rubbing herself lewdly against him, smiling widely with good teeth that protruded just a little, as she proudly held up one of his hands so that we could see his skinned knuckles.

'He got up when he hit the ground so I had to race down and hit the cunt again.' Fuggsi had dark shadows under his eyes like a man who didn't sleep well. In the firelight they looked as if they had been smudged with coal.

'What does Fuggsi do to earn a living?' I whispered to Leroy.

'What it takes,' he answered with pride. 'He a Moree boy.' Leroy pronounced Moree hard, and as two separate words, like banging something twice with a hammer when one hit would do. Fuggsi looked at us and grinned.

We got two houses that night, but they were only crowds to survive on. It was like eating Vegemite without the toast. Brophy had taken the easy money.

Michael had to wait until Brophy's show was over before he could start spruiking ours. He had to judge the crowd to perfection and spruik until the reputations of our fighters became more than worthy. Until he had fired up enough of the crowd into a fever.

Time and again he ordered the boys off the board and into the tent to start fighting, only to bring them back up in the hope of bringing in more paying customers when the flush of a new crowd appeared. Scourge and Leanne were kept busy guarding the entrance against gatecrashers. The showmen, who were always there to help Michael, kept the mugs already inside under control.

Michael put Kassi on the board. 'If you want to travel with us, eat our food, you pay your way,' he told her.

Again there were no big men. Bundy was kept down amongst the crowd and then matched against Mauler, who cracked Bundy's skull open with his own head during the fight. It was a wide wound but not deep.

Black Snake showed he could fight as well as any we had had standing on the board. Chippie, breathing heavily, shuffled through another bout still holding his hands in a crooked peek-a-boo style, a surprised, stunned look coming to his face each time he was hit.

Skinhead turned up again and was beaten soundly, and then fronted up to fight in the next house, and was soundly beaten again. But each time he was knocked down, he got up ready to fight. We couldn't find a girl to fight Kassi.

Fuggsi's opponent was a rodeo cowboy. It was a wild swinging affair, and I was surprised that the stranger got the better of the fight. It finished when the shoulder of Fuggsi's opponent popped out of its socket, leaving his arm hanging limp and unusable by his side. A bull rider's affliction, I later heard.

When Michael and I got back from the Hole in the Wall, the boys were still drinking around the fire. They had placed the armchairs and the lounge within the reach of the heat, and draped themselves over the furniture like pashas in a harem.

Black Snake stood as we approached, and handed us two beers from a crate that was nearly empty. Mauler left to take a piss.

'*Vaya con dios*,' Fuggsi said to him.

'Don't go pissing around any of the caravans,' Michael warned him.

'You speak Spanish?' I asked Fuggsi.

'Jail talk. We always use Spanish. "*Adios*", "*hombre*", words like that.'

'Not when I was there.'

'Leroy, you was there a long time ago, man, it was a lot different then.There weren't no gangs in your days.'

'I've been in since,' Leroy answered, sounding insulted. I knew it had only been for fighting.

'Man, now there's Lebbos, Whites, Vietnamese, Murris. You got gang fights, stabbings, all sorts of shit goes on now. They got to keep ya separated.'

Leroy stood, stretched like a waking dog, and bludged a cigarette off Black Snake. 'In the old days, Aboriginals and whites stood together against the screws.'

'Not now, man, now screws keep a distance.'

'When I was there, the bastards would throw cold water over you on winter mornings.'

'They do that now and they'd get killed,' Fuggsi said.

Leroy seemed not to hear. 'We had a sit-in one time, and they bashed me.' And when he said Cessnock jail was the best he was ever in, I smiled like the proud father of a baby, because it was my hometown jail.

'What's your number, Mauler?' Fuggsi asked when he returned.

'Where's the beers, Snake?' Mauler asked before answering. 'Two hundred and twenty-seven.'

'Mine's hundred and seventy-four. Don't matter what jail you go to you always keep the same number,' he said to me, as if he were a soldier proudly telling me his dog tag digits.

'Bundy, you been inside?' Fuggsi asked.

'Yeah, just for not paying fines though. They caught me fourteen times for drink driving.' He reached up and felt his head gingerly. Blood had caked on the wound that Mauler had accidentally given him.

'And you, Snake?' Fuggsi asked again, as if it were an examination.

Black Snake stood and handed us another two beers from a crate that had miraculously appeared. 'Same as Bundy, just traffic tickets.'

Skinhead and Chippie wandered up to the fire so quietly that at first only Michael noticed them.

'Where you boys been?' Michael asked Chippie, but he was busy begging a cigarette from Black Snake and a hit of yanni from Leroy, and didn't answer. Then they walked back into the darkness.

'I'm taking Skinhead with us.'

'He can't fight, Michael,' I said, 'and another thing, Chippie was talking to him, he's on the run.'

'What did he do?'

133

'Bashed a kid's head in with a chain. They had him in a boys' home and he ran. He's still got six months to serve.'

'I think he'll be another Water Boy,' Michael answered, seeming not to hear.

'Who's buying the beers?' Michael asked me, suddenly giving all his attention to the bottle he held with both hands.

'Black Snake, he just got an insurance pay out from a car accident, it's burning a hole in his pocket I reckon.'

'Generous bloke,' Michael said seriously, 'but then they all are. When one's got something they'll share it all right, but mostly nobody's got anything. That's the shame of it.'

'Well, he keeps giving me money to look after for him, so I reckon he's doing his best to keep some of it.'

'He won't,' Michael answered with finality.

The next morning I got back from my run to an empty camp. There was no coffee being heated, nobody to watch the sun rising with, to talk quietly to, to share memories with. I looked around expecting to see empty beer cans, unwashed dishes, the detritus of revelry, but only found cold ashes in the bottom of the drum as a sign of the party the night before. It was Fuggsi.

I had coffee brewing by the time Michael came out of the caravan. It was always a little disconcerting to see such a large man, hair unplaited and dishevelled, coming out of such a small space. Like watching a bear leaving his winter cave.

'Where's Mikey these days?' I asked, when he came over to join me.

'Staying with Mandy's brother. They like having him around.'

I just nodded, staring blankly, while Michael scratched his head and pulled at his hair to untangle it.

'You've met him,' Michael said, when he realized I didn't understand, and I nodded again, trying to remember if Mandy, or anybody, had told me her brother was working the run.

Michael was sipping gingerly at the coffee that I always made very hot when I asked him who we were taking to Mackay? 'Black Snake, Fuggsi and his girl. Bundy reckons he's gunna drive up.'

'Bundy likes the company,' I said. 'I wonder what his family make of it?'

'Don't matter, when these blokes want to go, they go.'

'And Skinhead?'

'Yeah, I told you that last night. You don't like him, do you?'

'He can't fight, and he's a bad kid. He's trouble.'

'I'll teach him to fight. He'll stick, you'll see.'

'Just like Water Boy?' I answered sarcastically.

'Yeah . . . just like Water Boy.'

Scourge walked into camp before we had finished our first cup and told us about the trouble in the pub across from the show ground. A girl had been dancing on a table near the jukebox and a bartender had pulled her off. Scourge said that she scratched one of his eyes out.

'They have to learn that we can't be stood over,' he added.

When I asked Scourge whether that meant we would be barred from the pub, he told me that we could use chairs on them and still get in. 'Do you know how much money we spend in there?'

Michael stood up suddenly and impatiently. 'Get up, we got to go to work,' he yelled into the trailer.

Chippie, Mauler and Leroy stumbled out. Kassi, wrapped in blankets like a mummy, stayed lying on her cot, only pulling the covers back long enough to be identified. But only until Michael discovered she was there.

We were hung over, short handed, and needed half the day before we finally hoisted the tent into the trailer and packed up the last of our camp. While Michael tinkered with the Kenworth engine, I hitched the trailer onto the Ford, and we waited the word to move further north.

Fuggsi's car was large and unremarkable, but its noise, a low powerful rumble, made it easily recognizable. We all looked up when we heard it. It came fast across the grounds scattered with the woebegone ruins of the show that was in the process of moving on.

Kassi raced towards the car that raced towards our camp. 'Fuggsi's back,' she yelled for her own pleasure, just before she turned and sprinted in the opposite direction.

The car chased her, but was forced to pull to a stop, hindered by the trucks and caravans that stood ready to roll.

'You fuck'n' white cunt,' the Aboriginal woman yelled out after Kassi, as she pushed the car door open before it had come to a complete stop. 'I'm gunna give you what Fuggsi gave me, ya fuck'n' cunt.' But the woman was almost twice Kassi's age, and had no chance of catching her. Leroy and Mauler tried to calm her because they knew her well. She was a Moree girl, Fuggsi's childhood sweetheart, the mother of his children.

'Fuggsi give me a belting, and I'm gunna give that cunt the same.'

Leroy and Mauler eventually managed to comfort her into normality, and then she left. Neither Fuggsi nor Kassi returned to travel with us.

Michael gave Leroy, Black Snake, Mauler and Chippie an advance, and sent them off to have a drink while he continued to tinker with the truck. I thought it was a mistake.

They drank six beers before it was time to leave, and bought a carton of stubbies for the trip. The boys rode with me; Skinhead, who had finally turned up, rode with Michael and Mikey in the Kenworth.

*

It was late in the afternoon when I pulled out of the show ground and followed the Kenworth out of Rockhampton and onto the Bruce highway, heading north towards Mackay, 300 kilometres away. Once outside the city limits, Michael powered up the big truck and pulled away.

The old Ford, lugging a caravan and five men, had never been able to keep up. After twenty kilometres Michael was out of radio contact and we were alone, driving into a setting sun that filled the car with piercing light, forcing Leroy who was sitting in the front seat beside me to cover his eyes with an arm and complain bitterly that the beer was getting warm.

I shuffled my bum lower and squinted through Fuggsi's mercifully clean windows, noting during periods of respite, when rounding bends or passing in the lea of a hill, that the cattle grazing in the paddocks appeared crimson. Before we reached Marlborough one hundred kilometres up the road, it was night and the madness had set in.

'I got to take a piss. Stop the car.'

'There's no place, Leroy,' I told him. 'Wait until I see a good spot to pull over.'

But Leroy couldn't wait and, under threat of pissing in the car, I was forced to pull the caravan on to the edge of the road, leaving it dangerously exposed to passing traffic. The boys piled out, urinating in unison.

Cars and trucks raced past us, catching the boys in their lights, blowing their horns and screaming out obscenities that were lost in the emptiness of the country. Further up the road, Leroy grabbed at the wheel when I didn't stop fast enough.

'You little white bastard, you got to keep the trailer clean,' Leroy's screamed suddenly, and for no apparent reason at Chippie. 'And help with the camp, ya little white bastard. Give me a cigarette!' he demanded, as if that were natural after such abuse.

An empty beer bottle, not the first, went flying out the window, landing safely, losing itself in the long grass that grew along the side of the road.

'Ain't got any, Leroy, and why are you calling me a white bastard? I don't call you a black bastard,' Chippie answered, not intimidated.

Black Snake had cigarettes, and handed them out like labourers' wages. I lit a cigar and wound up the window when the boys started complaining about the cold wind, resigned to driving the rest of the way in the air purity of a chimney.

'Cunts like you stole our land. It's because of you we've got nothing and have to suffer,' he screamed again after lighting his cigarette, and dropping the still burning match onto the floor of the car.

'Mate,' I said, 'Chippie isn't even seventeen, he hasn't had enough time to make anybody suffer.'

'Where's the beers?' demanded Leroy, not listening to me.

'Gone,' answered Chippie.

'You stole them, you cunt.'

'Shut up, Leroy,' Mauler told him, and he did.

'What's life like on the mission?' I asked Mauler, taking advantage of the quiet.

'Nothing to tell, people don't work much, and the kids don't go to school. Shit, when the bus comes around to pick them up, only three or four get on, and the rest run.'

'Education is the only way Aboriginals are going to make it,' I told Mauler, as if I were an expert and there was only one answer. 'There's no way back, you've got to get your kids to go to school, and then they can change what they reckon's wrong.'

'We never asked to live in your world in the first place,' Leroy screamed out in a voice that sounded like it had been filtered through water, surprising everybody because we thought he had been sleeping. 'You don't need education to live like we usta live. Why do we have to do things the white man's way?' It was quiet for another moment, and then another empty bottle went flying out the window, this time bursting on the apron of the road.

We stopped at a garage to fill up and eat, but the boys were broke. Even Black Snake was temporarily under funded.

'What happened to all the advance money?' I asked Chippie, and then got a breakdown of what six beers each, a carton of grog, and enough cigarettes to make it to Mackay cost.

A family of showmen pulled in behind us. 'I saw some Boongs pissing along the side of the road,' one said to me, 'and then I realized they were our Boongs.' He then gave a small laugh and, shaking his head, continued into the restaurant.

When we drove away, Leroy started again. 'If you don't shut up,' I told him, 'I'll put you out the car and leave you.' But he knew I wouldn't.

Black Snake, recognizing Leroy's ranting as that of a drunk good man, tried placation with soft tones, but that didn't work, and then Mauler punched Leroy in the back of the head.

MACKAY

The next morning I woke angry. Leroy was still sleeping amongst a dishevelment of blankets when I got back from my run. When I saw Michael, I told him about Leroy's behaviour and that I wanted to have a word with him. I asked Michael's permission because I didn't want to make unnecessary trouble: it was Leroy and Mauler carrying the weight of the tent, not me.

'Do what you have to do,' Michael told me.

I woke Leroy up, and called him a racist cunt. He stared at me vacantly through red filmy eyes. Suddenly feeling that I needed to show libertarian credentials, I added, 'I got a Miskito Indian foster daughter who's blacker than you.' And then he threatened to leave.

'What did you do?' Michael asked me when I told him.

'Do what you got to do, you told me.'

'Yeah, but not make him leave, we need him.'

I kidded Leroy, bent over backwards to be extra nice, but he wouldn't talk to me. I gave up then and ignored him. Fuck him, I thought, he won't leave without Mauler.

In Rockhampton I bought a radio for the camp, and on our first morning in Mackay, Leroy tuned in a Murri station. As we lazed around waiting for our sausage and eggs that Black Snake fried with delicate concentration, we listened to Aboriginal country and heavy rock.

Between the music, the alter ego of the presenter made an appearance: 'Super Murray says you kids have to go to school and get an education.' I looked at Leroy, waiting for an argument, but he said nothing.

The men sat glued to the station while I busied myself making coffee. Only when the sweet earthy fragrance of a proffered cup reached them, did they let their attention lapse long enough to nod a thanks.

We listened quietly as we drank: there was a discussion about violence in the home and another about the problems of excessive alcohol consumption, and then Super Murray was back telling the kids about the evils of glue sniffing. It was a good station, concerned and entertaining. The boys were proud.

The tent went up easier because of the extra hands, but we were still rough and without Michael it would have fallen down in the first breeze.

'When are you going to buy us that meal you promised?' Mauler asked, as he read an Aboriginal produced newspaper I had bought in Rockhampton. But before getting his answer, he said, 'Listen to this, "The Cherbourg state school principal Chris Sarra has been named Queenslander of the year." Hey, the brother would be Zac and Chris's teacher.'

'See what we can do when we're left alone?' Leroy said to me.

'When did I promise that, Mauler?' I asked, not bothering to answer Leroy.

'Rockhampton,' Mauler said and, not even looking up from the paper, demanded a cigarette from Snake.

I remembered vaguely that Mauler and Leroy had been talking about a restaurant called the Hog's Breath Cafe, a steak house chain. They told me they had seen it advertised on television, and even knew what they would order. That's when I told them I would take them out for a meal in Mackay.

'I want a surf and turf, it's a big steak with prawns,' Mauler said again from behind his paper.

'And what about you, Leroy?' I asked.

'Same,' he grunted, regretting immediately that he had spoken to me.

'But I don't remember inviting you,' I teased. 'Why don't you just go yourselves?'

'No money,' Mauler answered quickly, raising his shoulders at the same time, and then he said, 'Hey, listen to this. The Cherbourg council is bankrupt. Says here they are more than a million dollars in debt. Shit, them brothers ain't no better than us Moree mob.'

'Tonight we'll go and eat,' I relented, thinking it would bring Leroy around.

Mauler looked over the top of his paper smiling contentedly, temporarily flattening his nose and lengthening the scars over his eyebrows.

'You want to come, Snake?' I asked, and when he nodded I noticed a tattoo on his upper arm. He flexed his muscle when he caught me staring, giving me a better look at a black snake in striking position. Then he asked me for some of his money I was holding.

The boys made an effort to look good for the evening: Mauler shaved and put on clean jeans and a new shirt. 'Where did you get the shirt?' I asked him, admiring it.

'Snake,' he answered, neutrally, as if Snake was always buying shirts for him.

Leroy started speaking to me, but curtly. I asked to borrow his shoe polish and he asked to borrow my hair cream and toothpaste. Snake put on brand new black jeans, and a shirt with a yellow and red flame that he had bought with his insurance money.

*

The Hog's Breath Cafe was located in downtown Mackay, an area dotted with historical buildings and palm trees. A preened location, one where tourists could feel comfortable, which seemed to be the main consideration of most local councils in Queensland.

You entered the restaurant that was decorated with mass produced memorabilia and clutter through a small, sham saloon bar. Sadly, I thought about the great Australian pubs that didn't use any theme to bring in customers, and whose steak dinners were half the price. But novelty was a big seller these days, and the boys had bought into it.

When we were finally seated, I was looking directly at a picture of a jiving young Elvis Presley on the wall. A picture of Jimmy Dean hung on another. A jukebox that played rock and roll stood in a corner. We knew what we wanted and we waited. The restaurant was not full. Fifteen minutes passed and we had still not been noticed.

'It's because we're Murris,' Leroy suggested, agitated, 'that's why she won't serve us.'

'No, she's just busy,' I answered, looking at the girl who seemed to give attention to everyone but us.

Mauler and Snake stayed out of it, discussing the menu in detail as if they were part of a study group, dissecting and analysing a great novel.

'She don't like black fellas,' Leroy said again. His face, which could look like a small boy's with great expectations, became furrowed and concentrated. Snake and Mauler looked up from their discussion, and I sensed a slow conversion taking place.

'Excuse me, we've been here twenty-five minutes, and we'd like a beer,' I demanded, hoping to head off trouble.

The waitress apologized with sincere words in a gentle Irish accent. 'I'm alone,' she said.

'It's the fucking restaurant,' I told the boys. 'Not enough staff.'

A few minutes later, we were downing beers like labourers on a Friday arvo, but it was still another twenty minutes before the steaks arrived. She smiled at the boys, who still harboured suspicions when she brought them, spoke a few words in her sing-song enunciation and convinced them of her best intentions. A little later she came to ask whether we were satisfied, and Leroy answered her with words that were as sweet as if they had been battered in honey.

Restaurant fever had caused part of the tensions that night. I recognized it because I had suffered badly from it myself for many years. On occasions, I still did. Sons of coalminers, like Aboriginals, are not used to being waited on, or eating in public, or having to make a choice.

Leroy and Chippie jogged with me the next day. They set their own pace and returned enthusiastic. I thought then that Michael was getting together a troupe not unlike the one his grandfather had.

The boys had on the radio when we got back. During breakfast, which Black Snake again cooked, we listen carefully to an announcement of an action that was being organized. A convoy of cars was to be driven along a national highway in the Northern Territory at sixty kilometres an hour to make people aware of Aboriginal health and land issues. This caused nods of agreement and murmurs of assent from the boys, and then Super Murray returned to admonish the kids some more. When his theatre was finished, they played a Jesus ballad.

It was a song by Rodger Knox. I had met him years before in Joe Maguire's pub in Tamworth in NSW. Joe Maguire was big, tough, honest and egalitarian, and when he provided live entertainment, Aboriginal musicians appeared as often as whites.

I remembered Rodger, because I liked his soft thoughtful ballads, and because he gently, persuasively argued away some of my youthful ignorance about Aboriginals, and because he survived a plane crash, but not without consequences.

He had been flying between Aboriginal missions where he had been performing, when his plane went down and he was badly burnt. He was the only survivor. After being gone for so long, so many people had already died on me. So, I thought, you're still alive! I was cheered.

That same morning Karla, Michael's thirteen-year-old daughter arrived. It was school holidays, and suddenly the show ground seemed to fill with the high-school age offspring of the showmen. Michael introduced her to the men, and said, 'If anybody disrespects her, I'll kill them.' The boys knew he wasn't joking.

'Shake 'em up, shake 'em up. Hold da, hold da. Ladies and gentlemen, Les Darcy came into the audience hanging on his old mother's hand, and she was endeavouring to stop him from having a go for one of Bell's cash prizes. Little did she know, ladies and gentlemen, she was holding back one of the greatest fighters Australia and the world has ever known.' Michael swayed when he told the story, his voice shook with feigned passion, but the crowds were young, and I wondered would anybody know who Les Darcy was. 'We carry a big team of fighters, all weights and all sizes.'

Skinhead was again beaten badly, but not into submission. He was like a kangaroo I had once put bullet after bullet into. The roo stood erect, passive, almost disinterested, bleeding to certain death. It was admirable and if Skinhead would have had a blush of conscience or empathy, he would have deserved saving, but he hadn't, and he was on his way to hell.

Leroy landed a powerful, precise left hook, dropping his

opponent. The punch was a nugget from his vein of youth. All old men have these nuggets, the elements just have to be right before they can be rediscovered, shining and as valuable as ever.

Chippie shuffled through another bout, and Black Snake's opponent took an asthmatic attack. While we were waiting for the ambulance to reach us through the crowd, Michael had him sign a non-responsibility declaration form. He was breathing raggedly and painfully when he scrawled his name, unsure what he was signing, but there was no alternative. Litigation had become a sickness in Australia, and why would Michael be responsible when somebody decided as an adult, to take a risk in life? All local fighters were supposed to sign these forms before they fought, but try and explain that to testosterone-affected drunks.

The man Mauler fought was an Aryan. Huge and hard. The toast of the town. He lasted the three rounds, but only because Mauler allowed him to. He knew that keeping the public happy, as far as limits permitted, was the premise of Michael's tent boxing philosophy. Michael gave the fight a draw. The Aryan didn't even stop to collect his money. The trick had worked on everybody but him.

Scourge again complained to Michael that he shouldn't being so willing to pay the locals, and Michael again explained that it was the locals who brought in the paying public, and if you didn't give the public something to cheer, they were not going to come.

In Mauler's second fight that evening, he lost the plot, but you couldn't blame him. I was guarding the ladder, standing close to the mugs, when a young white man stepped forward with his hand up. His shirt was already off, his muscles were flexing, he was dancing up and down.

He had just gotten out of jail, he told Michael, and even above the boom of the drum and clang of the bell you could hear his boasts about what he intended doing to Mauler. He had brought his family. Brothers, father and uncles, who encouraged his bravado, prideful of their family representative.

It was like watching a nail being thumped in quick succession by two hammers. Mauler gave the jailbird no quarter, and bludgeoned him into retirement. I had never seen such ruthlessness in all of his fights.

'You know you could have brought us trouble with the crowd, you know that, don't you?' Michael said anxiously to Mauler.

'Sorry, Michael,' Mauler answered, breathing heavily, sweating badly, shoulders still hunched, pacing back and forth, and back and forth. 'He had a big mouth. He reckoned he was gunna kill me. Thinks being in jail makes you tough.'

Scourge's twelve-year-old son walked up to me as I was packing away the gloves and gowns. 'Why don't you fight, Wayne?' He said it respectfully, almost imploringly, and when I mumbled pathetically about age, he told me straight out, 'There are plenty of old fellas out there who want to have a go.'

We were walking to the Hole in the Wall, when Scourge suddenly changed direction. A couple of teenage mugs were sliding down a rubber dip that had been closed for the night. Michael and I watched in amusement while Scourge waited until they both reached the bottom of the long yellow rubber slide, grabbed them by the hair and yanked them outside the fence surrounding the slide, kicking their backsides as they stumbled away.

'Cunts could rip it or anything.'

When Scourge was buying the beers, I asked Michael about the tent's location. 'Yeah, it's all right. About time. Tickets are working good too. Still not making money though.'

'Do you want me to take over as camp boss?' I asked him, not because I wanted the job, but because I still felt I wasn't doing enough.

'You got to be able to knock out anybody to be camp boss,' Michael replied. 'And you can't.'

I was food shopping the next morning, carrying bags of groceries, when I passed a pub. When I heard my name called out, I thought it was meant for another Wayne. Then it was repeated.

I walked into the pub and saw Mauler standing in the middle of a group of men. He was drinking a beer and appeared calm enough, but his darting eyes and that excited voice he has gave him away.

'This bloke wants to kill me,' he said, pointing to a smallish, drunk man in his sixties, who only had one eye.

'Fucking boong,' the man with one eye said.

'Shut up, Bill,' the publican, who was standing behind the bar warned him.

'Fucking boong,' Bill said again, staring at Mauler.

'Finish your beer, Mauler,' I said, 'and if anybody wants to see this bloke fight, come down to the show grounds and front up at the boxing tent. He's our star fighter.' But nobody said anything.

'What was that about?' I asked when we were outside.

'I asked him what happened to his eye, and then he told me a fucking boong shot it out. So I told him I was a fucking boong, and then he wanted to fight me. A bit later, he said he would shoot me.'

Mauler had called me inside because he didn't want trouble and because he didn't want to hurt the man. That was Mauler, just a pussycat.

'I want to leave,' Mauler then said to me. 'I don't want to fight any more, I'm losing it.'

'You'll be right, Mauler,' I answered him, completely taken by surprise, and left it at that.

'Did you talk to him, Michael?' I asked later that same day.

'Yeah, he wants to leave, and if he goes Leroy will go too,' Michael answered in a voice that betrayed disappointment.

But I knew he wouldn't dwell on it, it was just a detail. Sometimes I thought of Michael's life as a bag of marbles, each marble representing a detail, and no matter how important the detail, it would quickly lose its place on the top of the bag and slide into obscurity amongst the other marbles, and another detail would take its place. In the showman's world of infinite change, it was the only possible way of moving on.

Fuggsi and Kassi turned up that afternoon in Fuggsi's car. Kassi sat close, holding tightly onto his arm, smiling widely, exposing her good, slightly protruding teeth. It was like a king returning with his queen. The camp greeted them enthusiastically, memories of her indignant flight and the pain that Fuggsi's wife must have endured seemingly forgotten.

Fuggsi had an authority over the others that I didn't quite understand. He wasn't a great boxer, not even a good one, and he wasn't big. He was tough, but realistically, although he might have beaten the others, he could never beat Mauler. Not in the ring nor in the street, and yet Mauler was as committed a devotee as the rest.

He was a success story, and that could have been the reason; he had a big fancy house, a car, an eight hundred dollar telephone. He was disciplined and decisive. But I was sure it was the disquiet he caused in others that gave Fuggsi his advantage. Fuggsi was badder, and everybody knew it.

He wasn't naturally bad, but he could become bad, and when he did, anything could happen. He would fight until he died, or you did. And he had a keen sense of grievance.

It was a madness, and I felt sorry for him because I knew he battled it, and when he could manage to win this internal fight, however short lived the victory, there was no one better.

Bundy turned up that day as well. I had just decided to move out of the trailer and into the Kenworth's cabin, when he walked casually into camp.

I knew he would come. It wasn't the money or the fighting that made him leave his family and join us. He needed to move, and he liked moving with us. It was a Murri thing, but whether that also applied to Murri women, I couldn't say.

'Give us a hand will you, Bundy?' And we carried a couple of quickly packed bags and my swag out of the mess that Chippie, Mauler, Skinhead, Leroy and Black Snake were living in. To be fair, Leroy and Snake were battling to keep order in their space, but were losing the fight to the others. Fuggsi would sort them out.

Michael called the cabin, 'The Hotel Kenworth'. It was nothing more than a cramped, draughty tin bunker, bolted precariously on behind the truck, and when it rained, water seeped through broken welds and ripped corners. Boards had been cut and fitted together over storage drawers, making a shelf that you could lay your swag on. Each morning I dismantled the shelf to make sitting space. It was impossible to stand.

It was the last day of the show and by late afternoon the crowds had started to dwindle. Michael called us together and tried to pull one last house out of Mackay. Bundy filled in as our heavyweight, because Mauler went missing, and Fuggsi took over Leroy's job on the drum when he didn't show up.

It was a poor house, and both the public and local fighters were the dregs of Mackay's show-going crowd. The bouts were scrappy and roared on by a young public who only relished barbarity.

We packed up at dusk and in haste. Thumbs and fingers were caught between steel pegs, fighters narrowly avoided falling tent poles pulled down without planning. Michael was too slow to move, and caught a pole squarely on the mouth, chipping away half a front tooth. Cries of pain and tirades of general abuse and profanity accompanied the work, but it was finished quickly.

We drove out through the show ground in the moonless early night. We were almost at the gates, when Mauler and Leroy, both panting badly, came running alongside the truck.

Michael told them to get into the trailer and sleep it off. For a moment I didn't think he was going to stop.

PROSERPINE

Proserpine, a sugar mill town, was just a two nighter. Three hours of dark driving to get there, but we still had time for a beer before bed. When I took a look at Proserpine in the daylight, I found it undistinguished, a working man's town under the eternal Australian sun. Perhaps that's what made it so friendly.

We put up before lunch. The large open show-ground bar was within sight and sound of our tent. You couldn't have a better location. The bigger rides had chosen not to come, but that was only to our advantage: more money left in the pockets of the mugs to spend on other attractions . . . on us.

Michael was elegant, persuasive, relentless. Moving the microphone from hand to hand like an amateur juggler. 'Plenty of spills and plenty of thrills. There's been a lot of enquiries from local fellows wanting to have a go. But you understand if you get knocked out, you'll have no claim on the prize.' 'Shake 'em up, shake 'em up,' and the drum and the bell could be heard all over the showground.

We filled the tent twice that first night, and the crowd was so thick they had to lean on each other's backs to get comfortable. There was no room to turn, barely any to twist. Each house was worth five thousand dollars in gate takings. That was a living.

Karla was put to work with Leanne selling tickets. Michael was slowly taking back control of the finances.

Mauler went missing again. 'Go and find him, Wayne,' Michael told me, 'and tell him if he doesn't want to fight, he can piss off. Fuck'n' not going to feed him when he won't fight.'

The show ground wasn't big, and I moved about it carefully, searching every corner, asking everybody about Mauler. The bar area was the toughest, because it was so big and it seemed to me that every man and half the women in Proserpine were drinking there. I wanted to find him because I knew Michael meant what he said. Mauler was our Take, the best we had, we couldn't afford to lose him. Besides, I thought, he didn't have much to go back to. I couldn't find him.

The first house was mostly lighter fellows, some solid boys, but only one big bloke. Michael gave him to Black Snake, telling the Proserpine fighter, 'My man's not gunna worry if you're a little bit heavier.' By the time we had filled up the second house, Mauler had returned, but refused to fight.

'I could see you looking for me,' he said, as if it had been a game of hide and seek. 'I was sitting on the log at the back of the bar.' Then he became unsure, serious. 'I can't fight, Wayne, I've lost my heart.'

'But nobody has beaten you, Mauler, you've never been hurt. It's just the grog and yanni.' Mauler nodded, shaking a little, looking like a frightened kid, unable to hold my stare.

'Keep him away from me,' Michael said, before he started spruiking the second house.

When the big bloke climbed the ladder, Michael put an arm around his shoulder, asked his name, was he a local bloke, and what he did for a living.

Then he said to the Proserpine sugar-cane worker, 'You're gunna have to fight me tonight, keeping in mind that if I knock you out, you're not gunna get paid.'

'And what if I knock you out?' the sugar-cane worker replied, bringing a smile to Michael, exposing the broken tooth, making Michael appear bad. Boom ba boom ba boom ba boom.

When all the fighters were matched and the tent full, Michael went down to change into fighting gear and Scourge took over the microphone duties. His commentary was stunted, but he had learnt the patter and handled it well. A newcomer, a swarthy, solid man wearing a black cowboy hat worked the corners along with the showmen.

'Who's he?' I asked Michael as he slapped his gloves together and threw some big air punches to get his arms working before going out to fight.

'An escape artist and a magician. His name is Frankie. Keep an eye on your watch if you shake his hand.'

Michael hadn't trained. He'd hoped not to have to fight, but he had no choice, our Take had quit. Michael was stiff and moved mechanically, but he was still strong and punched hard, swinging big left hooks like an axe man. The local bloke stayed with him, landing well, staying out of danger. Michael won the fight clearly.

'We'll pay the local fighter,' Scourge called out to the cheers of the crowd when the fight had finished.

Whenever we went for a beer in a local pub we took off anything that could distinguish us as being part of Bell's. It was necessary, because some locals made sport of having a go at strangers, and if there were enough of them, assuredly at ones belonging to a boxing troupe. If trouble happened, Michael didn't want any discredit brought on his family name, or give the police a clear way of tracking him down. But everybody recognized Michael when we walked into the Proserpine pub.

We had just meant to buy some cans and take them back to the boys, but we always lingered.

'See that bloke standing over there?'

I had just lifted my beer from the bar and had to turn to get a clear look at the big, darkish fellow standing near the pool table.

'He told me he was a Brophy fighter, so I told him to come down and we would show him how good Brophy fighters were.'

'He didn't show?' I asked.

'No, he didn't,' Michael answered ominously.

I took a gulp from my beer, knowing instinctively what Michael was about to say. Thinking it would be my only drink in that pub.

'If he says one thing, I'm going to get into him. No talking!'

I nodded, sure that this bloke had plenty of mates. I looked around for any other showmen who could back us up. Hoping Mauler, Aaron or Scourge were there, but finding we were the only ones.

The big fellow looked over at Michael only once, and then even furtively. He left before I'd finished my second beer.

The rest of the evening we were caught up with locals who were grateful to be told new stories and have new faces tell them. Maybe it was because Proserpine is on the main road leading north, a stop off to somewhere else, a town that meets a lot of strangers. Or maybe we just ran into good blokes. That night was the first time I had noticed Islanders. We would meet a lot more moving north.

We left on the afternoon of the second day. Michael had waited around hoping to get another house, but the fighters and fight aficionados of Proserpine were night people.

We picked up extra boys. Chris, a big round-faced, sixteen-year-old orphan, who lived alone in a cheap motel room, Bus, a wild swinging depressive hyperactive, who'd got his nickname when a bus ran over him, and Stretch, a tall, handy-fisted kid whose father fled Australia after a big dope deal went wrong. Lost white boys looking for a home.

Skinhead disappeared after he was bashed in a pub by a showman for disrespecting his girlfriend. A 'Water Boy' gone.

Before we left Proserpine, I drove to Chris's motel, a low simple building broiling in the sun, to collect his bags. While Chris was packing his gear, the owner and a mate came to speak to me. He's got nobody they made clear to me, and I made clear to them that Michael would take care of him. When they waved goodbye it was with concerned looks on their faces.

BOWEN

Bowen is spread out like flung corn seed. The show ground had been banished to a bleak, dusty area miles from the town centre. An advantage to the location however, was that it was only a couple of easy kilometres to a beach, and the pub on the beach.

Michael allowed Mauler to travel with us when the Moree boy said he thought he would be all right in Bowen.

The first day in town was another ritual day: the showmen collected their families together, hooked their jet skis and speedboats onto their second cars, and headed to a quiet bay along the coast to picnic and play in the water.

Michael loaded six of us into the Ford and the rest into Bus's badly rusting old Holden, which exploded complainingly into life only after a befuddling combination of peddle pumping and choke correction, and we followed the showmen to their playground.

We stopped at a supermarket along the way, where Michael bought us cases of beer, ice, six fried chickens, four loaves of white sliced bread, a packet of butter, soft drinks, chips and chocolate for Mikey and Karla, because Karla loved chocolate. We were the only non-showmen.

It was a glorious, wasteful day, where nothing more than a

rejuvenation of spirit through the elixir of sun, sea, beer, and purposelessness is achieved. Michael borrowed a jet ski, and took each of the boys on a wild roller coaster-ride, bouncing over the small waves like a paper-flat skimming stone, belching out petrol fumes and peace-ruinous noise, eliciting gasps of raw pleasure and uncontainable exhilaration from his passengers. The environment is being ruined I thought, but it would recover.

The Moree boys, the inland tribe, seemed to enjoy it the most, as if the salted water was a draught of invigoration not found on the sandy river flats of the Gwydir.

'I'm cured,' Mauler loudly proclaimed. 'I don't understand what was wrong with me.' He then took a large swallow of cold beer. Chris, our big, quiet orphan, behaved like a puppy amongst doting children, basking in any kindness that came his way.

The party continued in the pub by the sea. The one the showmen returned to each year, where they were known and appreciated. A peaceful night, one where show staff mingled respectfully with the showmen, although most still chose to drink in the back bar. A self-imposed segregation it seemed to me, but prudent I supposed, when drinking may have elicited behaviour not to be tolerated by bosses who were in any case intolerant.

I partnered a showman, a Hole in the Wall drinker, in a game of pool against two staff. The showman and I were absorbed in conversation, taking no notice of the game that we participated in, confident the way the balls were falling that the game was ours. The showman loudly insinuated foul play, when one of the show staff sank the black ball, winning the game.

The winners, who I knew had been travelling years with the show, defended themselves carefully, ignoring the blunt accusations. Better to drink out in the back bar if you're staff, I thought, even if there was no pool table.

There is always some bastard looking for a fight in a pub.

The man with the broad shoulders and dark hair moved from tent boxer to tent boxer, bragging about how good he could fight, annoying everybody. But after such a brotherly day, no one wanted trouble, and everybody let it go. When he draped a long arm over Michael's shoulder, telling him he was a Brophy fighter, I thought the period of peace was finished, but Michael just smiled and turned his back to him.

The next morning I ran alone. Leroy and Chippie both deciding to stay in bed. A shame, I thought, especially for Leroy whose general health had improved to the point where he hardly had to spit or dry retch, and where he could box three rounds in comfort. Leroy was actually looking ten years younger.

When I got back, Fuggsi already had the new boys setting up the camp. Even our boxing bag that had not been used since Bundaberg was hanging, ready. Fuggsi handed me coffee as soon as I flopped onto the lounge.

'Where's the music?' I asked.

'Michael's kids got the radio,' answered Fuggsi. 'Be good to have it back.'

I nodded, not sure what I could do about that. 'Camp's looking good,' I said, vaguely watching the boys who were sweaty and dishevelled, as if they had been dragged out of a deep sleep and put straight to work. Which, I suspected, they had been.

'It will be, got to keep these boys working though. They're lazy boys.' When he said that, I noticed Kassi in the camp kitchen frying the sausages.

Fuggsi sat across from me as I drank my coffee, rubbing the dark patches under his eyes. The sun, which was already high, lit up his face, showing it to be pale and drawn. His fists were clenched tightly together.

159

'Something wrong?'

'My boy, Wayne,' he said nervously, 'he called just before you got back, they've put him in a home. They say he's got some emotional problems, but he hasn't. They've got doctors talking to him. He wants me to get him out.'

'How old is he?'

'Seventeen . . . I want to take him back to Moree. Do you think they'd let me?'

'The police are involved, aren't they?'

Fuggsi nodded. 'When I go back, I'll get him out.'

'They might not let you take him, Fuggsi,' I told him, but he didn't answer me. He didn't even look.

We put the tent up as quickly as might be expected with so many helpers, but the details that held everything together still alluded us. The rope knots and pole angles remained a mystery. Driving the tent pegs into the hard ground was a skill we never mastered well, and the tent walls never seemed to fit. Dennis and I had become proficient at laying down a good, tight, level mat, but Dennis was gone. Mauler and Leroy were our only experts. They could assemble the line-up board and hang the banners with dexterity. Luckily Mauler had decided to fight on.

It was late afternoon when we finished, and while some of the boys threw together a meal of canned stew and boiled potatoes, Michael pulled me aside and told me he was going to ask his brother Steven to fly up and show us how to put on a good gee fight. As we sat talking, Black Snake brought us sweet coffee and we both sipped the drink, blowing in unison when we found it too hot to drink comfortably, watching the sun falling lower. For the shortest of moments the rides and joints burst into a vivid field of colours, and then it was dusk.

'You don't need Steven,' I said. 'You just want to straighten things out, but you're too proud to say so.'

'No, Steven knows how to gee fight better than anybody.' I didn't believe him.

'Let's go to the pub,' he said.

'Can we eat first?' I asked. 'The boys have cooked.'

'Is that what you call it?' Michael answered, pulling at his tail, blinking, smiling widely. Things I realized I had stopped noticing.

'When are you going to get that tooth fixed?'

'I'm gunna have it filled with gold in Cairns.'

'Nobody will ever trust you then.'

'What's new?'

The pub was already in full swing when we arrived. Scourge's father, a mountain of a man, so big he took up two places at the bar, called me over.

'You want a beer?'

I nodded, watching Michael wander off towards the pool table. I noticed that the Brophy fighter was there again.

'How's life on the show grounds treating you?' he asked, finishing his near full beer in a two swallows.

When Aaron had asked that same question in Rockhampton, I had answered that it was a tough life and I still thought so. But it had become more. I reached into my pocket to pull my wallet out, giving myself a moment to think before replying. 'Not many better ways to live,' I finally answered, and then I asked him did he want another beer.

John shook his head, and turned to get the barman's attention. 'Don't get into a shout with me,' he advised amiably, 'you'd never keep up.' He then ordered a beer for himself.

When it arrived, he picked it up and drained half in one gulp, nodding seriously as he settled the glass back on the bar, the way you do when you've heard something that supports your view on things.

My answer to John's question wasn't a politeness. I was a

greener on the other side of the hill man. That's what had always kept me unsettled and incited me to keep moving from place to place like an adequately fed dog looking for more bones. Packing up camp and leaving for somewhere new came perfectly natural to me. Another thing, I was beginning to feel like I belonged.

And there was the extraordinary: working the show ground was like travelling with exotic plunderers who bewitched whole towns with their inhuman machinery that threw or spun you into an impossible exhilaration; mesmerized you with their games of chance; intrigued you with tents that hid exoticisms or offered you up opportunities to stand out from the crowd; befuddled you with noise, smells, and a palette of colours, and retreated after lifting your money, leaving you giddy with astonished contentment.

'Do you come and watch the fights?' I asked John after I had finished my musings.

'No, it's too disorganized for me. It's not the same as when Michael's pop had it.' John thought a moment, took another giant swallow. 'It's not really Michael's fault, he's got blokes coming and going all the time, you can't organize when you've got different blokes all the time.

'In the old days, they'd stick around, some of them for years. Now they've got it easy, the dole's seen to that. Before they had to work for their money.'

I finally finished my beer at the same time as John was gulping down his third. 'Two beers, please, mate,' I ordered before he could protest.

'Do you know old Roy never brought them into town until show day? He'd keep 'em all out on a river bank somewhere.'

'His Aboriginal fighters?'

'All his fighters. The white fellas too. Old Roy would give everybody who smoked a packet of tobacco a week and feed them on kangaroo, rabbit, snake, anything they could catch. The black fellas preferred that, not the white fellas though. Roy's wife would cook, and they had an old black camp boss who would thump anybody who got out of line.

'I can understand nobody wants to live like that today,' John continued, 'but Michael doesn't even train his fighters. You've got to keep on top of those boys. Old Roy would have them sparring and practising the gee fights until they were perfect. He'd even have them running beside the trucks as he drove into town. Michael hasn't got the patience. Another thing, old Roy wouldn't let anybody drink close to show time.

'Of course –' he hesitated, shaking his head ever so slightly '– in those days, black fellas couldn't legally drink anyway. Worst thing they ever did was change that law. Buggered a lot of people up.'

It was one of my disappointments. I knew that if Michael spent some time with Chippie and Stretch, or even Mauler and Leroy, he would have had fighters who could have stood in front of anybody, and he would probably get his Water Boy. But Michael couldn't be bothered.

'Michael reckons he's going to get Steven to come up and train the boys to fight gees,' I said, noticing the Brophy fighter hanging over Mauler's shoulder.

'Is he? I don't understand why he hasn't done it before this. People like to see biting and kicking and spitting, even if it is only clowning.'

'He reckoned it could bring trouble,' I said, watching Brophy's man leave Mauler and walk towards Michael. 'Reckons people are not used to it any more. He thinks it would make them crazy. He's worried about the tent.'

The big man straightened when I said this, and stood over me like a schoolmaster about to deliver a punishment. But he only meant to stretch.

His story began without preparation, as if the bubbles from his beer on their way back through the passage of the body had retrieved some piece of show history out of its recess where it had been stored and catalogued like important archives.

'We had a wild West show travelling with us. It was John Godfrey's family.

'You don't mean Pete's family?'

'No, no, it was another wild West show. Used to be a lot at one time. The one I'm talking about belonged to John's family.

'You know John Godfrey?' John continued, starting to show impatience. 'He's got the food canteen. The short heavy set bloke.' I shook my head, looking clueless. 'The one with forearms like Popeye.' I nodded then, because you couldn't forget those forearms.

'The idea was you had to ride a bucking horse for ten seconds to win some money. The same idea as the boxing tent.' I waited. 'Well, this Yugoslavian bloke rode it for about a minute, John Godfrey reckons it could have been more, but the tent boss was John's auntie, a sort of matriarch, and women don't like paying.'

I nodded, agreeing like a lot of people do who don't see any point in disagreeing, and asked, 'Serb or Croat?'

'What?'

'The rider, was he a Serb or Croat?'

'Just fuck'n' Yugoslav. Is there more than one type? Anyway,' John continued impatiently, 'this bloke's pretty mad, so he came back with a big mob of mates, and all of them buggers had knives. There was a mad fight and they cut the tent to pieces. But a lot of heads were cracked with tent poles that night,' John added, a satisfied look on his face.

'What about the tent?'

'Ribbons of canvas,' John answered, suddenly serious. 'There were a lot of brawls back a few years. Shit, one time a mob of mugs even drove past shooting at the caravans. They're quiet as mice today.'

I was surprised that it was Leroy who settled it with the Brophy fighter. Even from across the room, and looking through the bodies of the other drinkers, I could see Leroy's left-right-left combination landing cleanly, and the troublemaker's head snapping backwards three times.

The Brophy fighter was saved by men around him, who didn't want his flaying to disturb their drinking any more than necessary. He was put outside and sent on his way.

'I couldn't knock him out,' Michael told me later, 'not after the trouble at Gin Gin, so I told Leroy to get into him.'

'He did a nice job,' I said. 'Cleaned him up the way he deserved to be.'

'Yeah, he did us proud. Are you coming to the two-up game tonight?' Michael added, and then bought me a beer.

Except on Anzac Day, playing two-up is illegal. I heard the ringer call come in spinner, and watched dumbly as the pennies left the wooden kip and flew darkly into the air, spinning unmistakably in the blazing white light given off by naked bulbs that had been strung above a shiny blue mat.

When the ringer called tails, a man who I did not know bent down amongst the shuffling feet of people moving this way or that to collect their winnings or pay their debts, and picked up the fifty dollars I had laid over his fifty dollar note on the ground.

Because the spinner is obliged to bet heads, and only allowed to continue tossing the pennies until he loses, a new man was offered the kip. When the new spinner's bet of two hundred dollars had been covered, shouts could be heard around the ring from the men and women wanting to wager their own money on heads or tails with anyone so inclined. And when all bets were laid, the ringer called, 'Come in, spinner.'

'Be careful, they bet big here,' Michael warned me.

I smiled drunkenly back. 'Just one more bet, and then I'm finished. You're not playing?'

'No, I get into enough trouble as it is,' Michael answered, chewing on a steak sandwich, which were being given out for free.

'Do they play two-up every year in Bowen?' I asked.

'Yeah.'

'Another tradition?' Michael just nodded, his mouth too full of steak to speak.

I placed my bet, thinking more thriftily. 'Thirty on tails,' I called out, and a twenty and a ten were laid quickly over my notes.

'What happens if the police come?' I asked Michael.

'What are they going to do? You think they can beat a community as strong as ours?'

Michael left soon after, and I meant to, but when the spinner's bets had been covered, I reached into my pocket and pulled out more notes, yelling out loudly and clearly, 'I'll back tails.'

'Did you lose much last night?' Michael asked the next morning.

'More than I wanted,' I answered, rubbing my head, trying to knead away the throbbing that was jarring and continuous.

'Some blokes won thousands.'

'Others must have lost thousands,' I answered still rubbing my head as hard as I could with both hands, giving myself temporary relief.

'Make us a coffee will you, Chippie?' Michael asked, as Chippie climbed down from the trailer, entangled with a dishevelled, dark-haired girl who clung to him as if she were drowning. 'And no fucking sheilas in the trailer. Now you know why we don't play two-up all the time,' Michael said when he turned back to me. 'Too much money changing hands.'

*

We were quietly drinking our coffee when Mauler and Leroy walked up to Michael. 'We're leaving,' Mauler said. He and Leroy stood shoulder to shoulder, heads bowed a little, moving anxiously from foot to foot. And then Mauler added, 'I can't fight any more, I thought I was all right, but I'm not.'

'You leaving too, Leroy?'

'Yeah, Michael. We came together, and I think I should leave with him.'

'I'll take you in to find a bus in the afternoon.' Michael never begged. His phone rang then, and he stood and walked away, saying, 'Yes, Mum,' in his soft voice.

I bought a twenty-dollar cone before the boys left, and we smoked it in the trailer. Fuggsi, under instructions from Mauler and Leroy who knew my intolerance for yanni, packed a small amount carefully into the bowl, and handed it to me. I lit it awkwardly and inhaled like a suffocating man until the last of it turned to smoke and only the ashes were left. It was then refilled to its limit and the real yanni smokers took their turns.

Black Snake, Fuggsi, Bundy and myself, using what we thought was logical argument, all tried to persuade Mauler to change his mind about leaving. When that didn't work, we belittled him.

Mauler reacted passively to our insults, accepting them without reaction, and so we contented ourselves that there was nothing more to do and let the mood of fellowship and sensitivity encouraged by the yanni have its way. And in that spirit of fellowship, we all promised to meet up later in the year at an Aboriginal rugby league festival in Sydney.

'Me and Fuggsi will be playing for the Mungindi Grasshoppers,' Mauler said, handing me the bong, and warning me to only take one toke.

'I played for the Mungindi Grasshoppers thirty years ago,' I told

Fuggsi, and Mauler nodded when Fuggsi looked at him for confirmation.

'A little nuggetty fellow called Willow was captain.' I was slurring badly, and rocking back and forth as if the trailer was bobbing over small waves, but Fuggsi seemed to understand.

'Willow's my cousin, he's one of our mob,' Mauler yelled. But I wasn't surprised.

Then out of the blue, Fuggsi gave me his Grasshopper football socks as a memory of those days when I was a bank clerk in Mungindi, and played five eighth for the Grasshopper's rugby league football club before it was an all Aboriginal team.

'What are you going to do when you get back, Mauler?' Black Snake asked.

Mauler answered immediately. 'I'm going to stay in my house for a long time. Not even going to come out the front door. Later I'll look for work.

'I'd like to get my job back at the meat works, but no chance of that. I was stealing three hundred dollars of meat there a week until they strip-searched me.' He hesitated a moment, and then he said, 'I was a meat thief and still getting skinny.'

It could have been the yanni, or the puzzled look on Mauler's face, or the way he kept scratching at his unshaven jaw the way some people do when they're concentrating, but we all began to howl with uncontrollable laughter, falling about the place as if the trailer was being rocked by a violent earthquake.

The boys left with dignity, both dressing in their best and shaking hands all round, before sliding into the back seat of the Ford.

'Give us a couple of cigarettes, Snake,' Mauler demanded as the car started up.

As they drove away they both turned and waved, but it was hard to gauge their mood, because their faces were clouded in thick smoke. We had lost our take and two mates.

If Michael was worried that Mauler and Leroy had gone, he didn't show it, not even when we heard that Bundy had left in the afternoon.

Bundy told me once that he had six brothers and sisters, one of whom was a lawyer another a schoolteacher. One sister was the first Aboriginal to make sergeant in the Australian army.

Both Bundy and Black Snake, Rockhampton boys, were different. Neither obsessed over Aboriginal rights issues unless harangued by the Moree boys, nor did they, unlike the Moree mob, seem to consider themselves victims.

I thought at one time that Rockhampton may have been a more impartial town than Moree, or one that at least gave the benefit of the doubt. But Bundy told me a story once that dispelled this theory.

'When my sister got back to Rockhampton from the army, and for no other reason than she was a Murri, they wouldn't let her in a pub.' But the strange thing is, he told it without any outward signs of bitterness or anger. I could never explain this difference between Rockhampton and Moree Aboriginals. Just a different mob I suppose. Pity that Bundy's heart told him it was time to leave.

It was fruit pickers and fishermen who came to fight us in Bowen, and everybody else came to watch. The fishermen were tougher.

Bus banged his chest, jumped up and down and scowled at everybody. It was not clear whether it was his depressive or hyperactive affliction that encouraged this behaviour, but in any case, he fought as madly as he behaved, even landing some punches.

Chris showed he was as soft and sweet as he looked, but Michael noticed it quickly, shortening the rounds, ending his fight before he could get hurt. Chippie and Stretch stood their ground inelegantly, and both lost. Black Snake and Fuggsi were now our only reliable fighters.

Kassi boxed for the first time that night, punching fluidly, belting her shorter opponent around the ring, while still holding her mouth in the shape of an arousing smile. I was considering stopping the beating when, without warning, Kassi's opponent sprang at her. She caught Kassi in a headlock and attempted to bite and strangle her. It would have been murder if the local girl was strong enough. When I finally prised them apart, careful not to touch what I was not supposed to, Kassi was still smiling.

Before we left the next morning, the police paid us a visit. The night before, Stretch had gotten drunk in town, and on his way back to the show grounds, had destroyed a public bench. Michael paid for the bench and signed a paper taking responsibilities for his future behaviour.

'It will be taken out of your wages,' Michael told Stretch as he stood between Michael and the copper, head bowed, looking sick and genuinely sorry. 'And if you do anything as stupid again, Stretch . . .' But he didn't finish, he didn't have to.

'You're a lucky boy,' the copper added, before he nodded his head at Michael and walked away.

Chippie, Stretch and Chris drove with me to Ayr. I felt like their father. I stopped halfway at a petrol station for coffee, bacon and eggs. The boys ordered potato chips and chocolate. I thought it might have been a question of money, but when I asked, learned it was a question of taste.

It was a bright morning, still early enough to be cool, and the petrol station like so many in that part of the country was an isolated building standing amongst the sugar cane fields. A staging post between towns. A good place to find a moment's respite from the responsibilities of life, but the boys were soon bored and moved about restlessly.

'I didn't think Kassi would be able to fight,' I said to anybody who was listening, mopping up the yoke of my fried eggs with the last of my toast, wishing the boys would sit down and give me some peace. Realizing with certainty that I would have made a bastard of a father.

'Maybe she learnt in jail,' Chippie said to me.

'She's been in jail?' I asked, still chewing, taken completely by surprise.

'She just got out. A year for armed bank robbery. It was her boyfriend's idea, that's why she only did a year. Not Fuggsi, another boyfriend,' Chippie made clear.

'Has Michael ever been in jail?' Chippie then asked me.

'No, he hasn't. I heard him telling Skinhead before he ran off, that to be put in jail's a shame, not an honour. He said it don't make you any tougher, just badder. He's right, and don't you boys ever forget that.' Then I felt more like their father than ever.

I lit a cigar over the complaints of the boys and drove the rest of the way to Ayr smoking peacefully, listening vaguely to conversation I didn't really understand.

AYR

The Ayr showground was shunted in on four sides by sugar cane fields, as if the farmers had accidentally overlooked it, but it was only a matter of time until they realized their mistake. We waited hours for Michael to arrive, and when he did, discovered that he had blown a tire on the Kenworth, throwing rubber all over the road leading into Ayr, and almost tipping the truck over.

Scourge pointed us to the site which was right next to the show bar, the best possible spot, because drunks and fights went together like avarice and mistrust We put up the tent in our fashion, and then it was almost dark.

Snake and Kassi were sharing their kitchen talents, getting on better than I did with Leroy under the same circumstances, and Fuggsi had the boys tidying up the trailer again, when Michael asked me to give him a hand.

Michael had a new tactic for bringing in the public: Bell's Boxing Troupe posters taped to pub walls. In Australia, it's common knowledge that when a drinking man discovers that a boxing tent is in town by spying a poster over the rim of a half empty glass of beer, it piques more interest than any other method of advertising.

It has something to do with the relaxed and confident state of the mind caused by the swilling of alcohol, and the challenge that poster offers up. Put the two together, and at least until the drinkers sober up, you have more men ready to fight than you could ever need. And when men go to fight they take an audience with them, otherwise, what's the point?

It is also a catalyst for new conversation between old mates, and for the older drinkers, a nostalgic prodding, reminding them of the days when they would have answered the call of the poster without consideration. We drove around to half a dozen pubs, each one glad to hang up a poster.

The last pub we walked into was located between the town and the show ground, but a considerable distance from both. An old-fashioned working man's pub with a large horseshoe bar that let you see and converse easily with other drinkers across from you, if that was your want.

The owner was very old and badly crippled. He limped around the bar with difficulty but determination, and for somebody who seemed to be in so much pain, with humour and vast amounts of energy. Chatting and laughing constantly with his customers.

And, he had cleverly employed a young and pretty barmaid with jet black hair who flitted around the bar, giving the drinkers who were for the most part not young, another reason for coming to his pub.

It had been a while since Michael and I had drank together. He was often gone from the camp, coming back only when it was close to show time. His kids took up a lot of his time, but he also spent time with his mates, or driving around looking for things to buy and sell; trucks, cars, anything that looked like it had a profit in it. And now that money was finally rolling in, it gave him added impetus.

We ordered a couple of beers and two meat pies. The pies were old and dry, but we scoffed them down quickly because we were famished, and meat pies for Antipodeans can never truly be uneatable. The beers were as they should be, and we decided on drinking more than the two limit we had set ourselves.

Michael was chatting with the barmaid when his phone started ringing. I looked into my beer, taking no notice, but I could hear that it was Mandy. He turned slightly from me, giving her all his devotion.

Michael always surprised me. Listening to him talk to Mandy, it was as if he was another man than the one I'd just been drinking with. But I already knew he could be two distinct people: a free wandering soul with a greater purpose, or a contented, hard-working family man rooted in a tiny country town. It came to him as naturally as blinking.

Sometimes it went wrong of course, as if he woke one morning and half asleep forgot who he was supposed to be, and then he would hook a bouncer and be barred from the pub, or have some trouble with the locals. But that didn't happen often.

'I've got to get you a fight,' Michael said to me after he finished talking with Mandy. 'I've been waiting for the right bloke to put his hands up. Plenty of old black fellas out there. I'll find someone you can get into.' That was Michael trying to be sweet. He knew instinctively that I wanted to fight, and he knew I was scared to fight and why. That was his solution: find someone who couldn't hurt me.

At the beginning of the fourth beer, Michael broke into a rap song: 'Fight who said fight. Get out of my way. Big boys don't scare me . . . I'm gunna make it a hit,' he said, and I knew he meant it.

The bar next to the tent was full and rowdy, and offered up all the fighters and paying public we could handle. The rush and crush to buy tickets almost overwhelmed us. Michael had Karla and

Leanne selling tickets, and myself and Scourge standing behind them, checking and tearing the tickets so they couldn't be reused, and making sure that nobody snuck or pushed past the girls.

In the afternoon Michael had given Chris a haircut, shaving him close, roughening his appearance, and before our show started, he stood him by the tent entrance dressed in Bell's boxing gear to intimidate potential troublemakers. Nobody knew that Chris was sweet and soft.

We had three houses that evening, all full and edging on uncontrollability. During the first house, groups of young blokes and girls strolled confidently past the ticket sellers, but when I stopped them, Scourge told me they were show kids. 'Let them through,' he told me.

They behaved like young royals: cocksure and loud, but no different I suppose than any kid would whose father owns the company.

Stretch was taking a beating from a tough Italian kid, hands flung hopelessly in the air trying to block a melee of punches when he fell back into the crowd, spinning and falling forward as he did so. A mug caught him by the shoulders and lifted a knee towards his face but, jostled by the bodies around him, missed by millimetres. It was a full-blooded strike and would have broken facial bones if it had landed.

I pulled Stretch back out from amongst the crowd, before I punched his attacker. Before the mug had regained his balance, showmen had swarmed around him and were pushing him roughly out of the tent. Fuggsi then ran outside and hit him again.

Michael was furious. 'You could've brought the whole house down on us. What if he'd had mates?'

'The bastard lifted a knee into Stretch,' I said self-righteously, 'he could have put his nose through his brain.'

'Then you give me a signal, and I'll have some of the boys pull him under the tent wall and we'll give him a hiding outside. But we'll give him a proper one so he can't walk away and bring back a mob of mates.'

Michael was right, but I hadn't thought before I acted. The show grounds had changed me as well: before I'd always thought.

We broke the tent down after the last show and drove away after midnight. The show-bar was in its last jubilant death throes, the drinkers prolonging their celebration in the certainty that it would be another year before it could be repeated.

Police stood casually around ready to adjudicate any problem, and herd off the last of the stalwart drinkers when it was finally time.

A large mob of youths recognized us as we drove out of the grounds and waved to us as if we were a cruise ship pulling out of port. 'See yas next year,' one of them yelled, and then another said, 'See yas.'

Frankie the escape artist drove with me to Townsville. It was drizzling steadily and the rain clouds shut out any moonlight, leaving the countryside featureless. Only when we passed through the tiny, lit communities that jumped spasmodically out at you through the rain and dark, could you take your bearings, and place yourself on the road to somewhere.

Chippie, Stretch and Chris were snuggled together on the back seat like puppies around a mother's teat. I thought they were asleep and then I heard the crack of a match being struck and caught the glow of the flame in my rear-vision mirror. Before Chippie's smoke reached me on the front seat, he said, 'Fuggsi hit Bus when you and Michael were at the pub.'

I looked into the mirror and caught him inhaling, staring out the window into the blackness.

'What was it about?' I asked.

'Fuggsi's bossing us around all the time, we're sick of it, and he's always calling Bus stupid. Bus said something, that's all.'

'Not good for a manic depressive,' I answered more to myself than Chippie. 'Fuggsi's spent too much time in jail, Chippie,' but Chippie didn't answer.

Frankie, who was sitting next to me, tilted his hat upward off his large forehead with his index finger, wriggled out of his dozing position, straightened, and lit his own cigarette.

'Problems?' he asked.

'Dunno, might be,' I answered, wondering whether I should talk to Michael about Fuggsi.

I hardly knew Frankie. The last two shows he had helped us with every house, but I hadn't spoken more than a few words to him. I felt he had a terrible loneliness about him.

'When will you perform?' I asked, wanting to talk, needing a distraction from the road that was shimmering and endless.

'In Townsville. An assistant will wrap me in a straightjacket, and a crane will lift me thirty-five metres in the air by my legs.'

'And then?'

'I escape from the straightjacket.'

'Not scared?' I asked. 'I'd be pissing myself.'

He hesitated before he answered, and I thought I saw a grin, but I was concentrating on the road and couldn't be sure.

'I always feel best when I'm wrapped in a straightjacket and hanging upside down from a high place. It's the only time I'm really happy.'

'That's pathological, mate,' I said, only half joking.

He smiled, and this time I saw it clearly.

We drove along saying nothing for a time, the rain banging steadily onto the window, mocking the wipers that were old and slow.

Without warning, and almost joyfully, Frankie said, 'One time

177

I jumped off a bridge into a river wearing a straightjacket. It took me a lot longer to escape than I thought it would.'

'Crazy life you've got.' Thinking Frankie was a little bit nuts.

'I'm writing a book about it,' he answered, drawing on his cigarette, looking severely at me. 'It's called *Life's Many Deaths and Suicides.*'

TOWNSVILLE

We drove into town at 3.30 am and didn't see the famous rock that rose up like a cyst, splitting Townsville in two until the following morning. This was another big show, and all the major rides had turned up.

We put the tent up in fierce heat. We were now at latitude 19 13 S longitude 146 48 E 1300 kilometres north of Brisbane.

I tried to sleep after the tent was up, but was driven out of the Kenworth by a children's train ride that clanked loudly over winding, undulating rails laid only inches from the cabin.

I wandered around without purpose, but with the intention of ending up at the show-ring, knowing the horses would be jumping, and hoping to speak to some of the riders, many of whom had become friends. The excitement and happiness amongst the show's visitors was palpable and infectious as it always was in all towns.

This was an old-fashioned agricultural show where tractors, harvesters and agricultural accoutrements were still displayed for sale. Horses, breeding bulls and prize milking cows moped about stockyards. Poultry clucked in cages, and sheep were gathered in pens. The best fruit, vegetables, pies and cakes were displayed for judging on long tables as if they were the answer to the world's famine problems. Townsville show was still a country man's market.

I was carefully biting into a toffee apple, worried that I would break a tooth, when I saw the tent. At first I didn't recognize it, but then its blue and red stripes triggered my memory. It was the one Michael had sold in Rockhampton.

Exotic posters and captioned photographs covered its canvas walls and stood on the tables positioned throughout the tent as if for a banquet. It was a visual history of the show grounds.

'What do you think?' asked Richard.

I threw the toffee apple away before I answered. 'Beautiful.'

Richard was a zealous man, full of boyish energy. It kept him trim and fit, but never let him rest. He was sitting on a stool by the entrance when I walked in, and I had to stop and think if I had ever seen him sitting before.

Richard came every night to watch the fights and I had got to know him well enough. There were few people I had met who were as likeable, or who laughed as easily, or as much. It was only much later that I found out he was Darren's father.

'There were no night shows in the old days,' he told me as I pulled up a chair next to him, as if he were a paid guide at the exhibition instead of its creator. 'We'd show in the daytime, and vaudeville shows would take over at night. A lot of times a circus was also in town. Bullen's or Ashton's,' he added for precision.

'See that photo up there,' he said, pointing, 'that's how we travelled. All our trucks and caravans would be loaded onto trains. Roads were bad in the old days and in plenty of places you couldn't even get over the creeks. Sometimes there would be six full trains for the show and the circus. Six trains just for us.'

'Why did that stop?' I asked.

'Got too expensive and the rides got bigger. We couldn't fit on the trains any more.'

'Can I smoke?' I asked.

He nodded, wrinkling his nose up at the same time. The smoke from my cigar was hardly noticeable in the tent of wonders.

'Have a look around and let me know what you think, and if you want to ask something, I'm right here.'

'What about your rides?'

'I've got my people watching them.'

'Who's the naked woman?'

'Paula Perry, but she's not naked, she's wearing a G-string. Paula worked until she was eighty. Ended up performing at old people's homes. They called them leg shows; very popular. The Country Women's Association was always trying to close them down.'

I wandered around, bewitched by the posters that, in intense colour and ebullient design, promised all that could be imagined exotic by a country boy: Indians climbing ropes attached to nothing; vivacious, legless women; Salome the beautiful and exotic; the tattooed lady; fat ladies; bearded ladies; snake ladies; giant men; strong men; African pygmies; Chinese pin heads; fire walkers; the globe of death; mice, monsters and fleas; an assortment of the deformed. It was all there.

I turned and walked back over to Richard. 'Peter Gill called those freak shows,' I said, pointing in the direction of the posters.

Richard, who had been gazing outside, twisted on his chair, looked up at the posters and smiled. 'It's just a name.'

'Yeah, that's what Peter said as well. What happened to them?' I asked, waving my hand in an arc, trying to wipe away cigar smoke that drifted thickly near Richard's head.

'They just moved away after the show societies closed them

181

down in the fifties,' he answered, not seeming to notice the smoke that had floated around him like a pea soup fog.

'But why were they shut down?'

'The show societies were frightened of the do-gooders, and the do-gooders were convinced those people were being exploited. I never understood it, where were they supposed to work if not here? They were making a good living.'

I had already turned my attention to a photo of men standing in front of a tent wearing cowboy hats and holding guitars, when Richard said, 'I wonder if the do-gooders ever gave them people some work.'

'What about these blokes?' I asked, pointing to the musicians.

'Don't you recognize him?' Richard asked, and when I shook my head he told me it was a photo of Slim Dusty.

Slim, who was our most beloved country and western singer, had died a few months earlier. They played his most famous song, 'The Pub with No Beer', at his funeral service, and most of Australia was listening.

'Tex Morton was another,' Richard continued. 'We even had rock and roll singers. You remember Johnny O'Keefe and Normie Rowe?' I nodded. 'They both travelled with us.'

I continued studying the old photos, slowly understanding the enormity of the show's importance to country towns: the machinery for sale, the livestock and agricultural produce on display, the innumerable tents that hid all that could be imagined. The images of the showmen and their staff: the singers, fighters, exotic dancers, animal handlers, ride and joint operators, cowboys, daredevils, freaks. The trains that carried them all into the heart of our country.

'We were their only entertainment,' Richard said, jolting me out of my concentration. 'Now people are spoilt. Television's seen to that. The only thing that excites them now is the rides. At least that's what the kids want, and they've got the money these days.'

'Yeah, that's what Pete said.'

I walked out of the tent with Richard, leaving a thin trail of blue smoke, and when we reached his brightly painted kiddie's rides, I stopped to say goodbye.

'Still, a show like this brings twenty thousand extra people to town. That's a lot of extra money coming in, and that means we're still important,' Richard said, grabbing my shoulder tightly, making sure I didn't leave before he had finished. I nodded in total agreement, and walked off into the crowd.

Before our first night show, I watched a team of speed car drivers race powerful white vehicles around the dirt show-ring track, throwing up storms of dust that settled thickly on hair and shoulders. They made me forget time.

When I got back to the tent, Michael was already on the line-up board testing the audio equipment. I looked unconsciously up at the Ferris wheel and the gondolas were full.

'Wrong sort of people,' I said

'Got to try,' Michael answered.

'Is Steven coming?'

'Reckons he's too busy.'

'Shame.'

'Yeah, nobody fights gees like him.'

'Shame for both of you,' I said.

Chippie was our drum beater and Stretch was on the bell. They held the beat, but I missed the brevity that Leroy put into his pounding and the principled, dignified stare that he gave the crowd with his dark ancient face, which he slowly twisted left to right and back again.

The first two sessions were a regression to the bigger cities back south. Just young street kids swinging, kicking, and trying to steal

183

into the tent without paying. In the last session, Bus took some particularly hard wallops.

When Michael and I got back from the Hole in the Wall, I walked over to the fire that the boys had built. Since Mauler, Leroy and Bundy had left, the camp had turned almost dry and the boys were talking quietly. A couple were sipping cups of coffee, but I didn't notice any alcohol or yanni. I checked that there was contentment and climbed up into the Kenworth hotel. It was only a few minutes later that I heard the rising voices.

I caught the last movement of a punch, saw Bus stumble back but remain standing, and then all was quiet.

'What's going on?' I asked, climbing down awkwardly from the truck, but nobody wanted to say. Fuggsi, who had thrown the punch, squatted on a log near the fire, looking towards the ground. Bus turned and walked to his car and then drove slowly off through the show grounds.

'Let's get some sleep,' I said, and climbed back into the Kenworth.

The camp was quiet enough the next morning. Bus had returned and Fuggsi was again organizing the boys in camp containment. Snake was cooking breakfast. I stretched, thinking I should start running again, and then I tried to remember the last time I had, but it was too many shows ago.

'I've got to leave,' Snake said to me as I walked over to him and pinched a piece of freshly made toast, all thoughts of running gone. 'I've got to take care of some things back home, but I'll come back,' he promised. 'And I won't leave until after Townsville's finished.'

'Have you told Michael yet?'

Snake shook his head. There was always a reluctance I noticed from the boys to tell Michael something that could make him mad.

184

'Better tell him soon,' I said.

Snake nodded glumly before asking, 'You got that money I gave you to look after?'

That evening, I watched Frankie perform. He appeared in the show-ring in front of the main grandstand wearing an evening suit and seeming larger than I remembered. He calmly gave his black cowboy hat to a glamorous young female assistant, and then the girl, who was also dressed in a formal gown, wrapped him like an Egyptian mummy in a straightjacket, double-checking that he was tightly buckled. Frankie then lay down flat, allowing his feet to be bound by straps that were attached to chains, and was hoisted high into the air by a crane.

An overweight presenter with a powerful gravel voice, and a flair for theatrics, stood by the crane and kept the crowd, which was large and appreciative, informed about the dangers and skills needed to complete the trick safely.

Frankie writhed and bucked for a few minutes and then an arm came free. In a few moments more, his straightjacket was hanging off him like the shirt of a drunken brawler. When they lowered him it was to immense applause, people crowded around, and I had never seen him happier or less lonely.

That night Fuggsi refused to fight. He had hurt his shoulder in a bout in Ayr, and reckoned it needed rest. Michael didn't like excuses, but let it go. He used Chris instead, and told me to referee his fight.

'Talk to him in the corner and make sure he holds his hands up. Just tell him to keep himself covered,' Michael said with real concern.

I nodded, and walked to where Chris sat while showmen laced up his gloves. 'Michael won't let you get hurt,' I said. 'Stay behind your gloves and keep moving.'

The crowd had been driven into distraction by the previous fight: a local Aboriginal against Black Snake. A fine fight, fast and furious. No quarter was given.

When Chris stood up to fight, they were baying for more blood. It took just one punch from his big mature opponent, a right hand to the forehead, and Chris was finished. When the punch landed, Chris wobbled but remained upright, looking at me like a dog who's been kicked hard for incomprehensible reasons.

'Take him to the corner,' Michael said into his microphone.

As we undid his laces, Chris was apologizing. 'I was out on my feet,' he said in a broken voice filled with contrition. 'I could hardly move.' Everybody understood and forgave except Chris himself.

'Ladies and gentlemen, we are looking for another opponent for the local boy. Who's willing to step up and have a go?' Michael asked three times, and when nobody volunteered, I said, 'I'll fight him.'

The first knockdown was a heavy loping right hand. I climbed back to my feet and went after him. I was knocked down two more times over the next three rounds.

'Why didn't you punch and move? Why did you stand in his face? He was way too big. I thought you'd punch and move,' Michael said with exasperation.

I stood listening, but both ears were cut and swollen, and his voice sounded like a buzz that was far away. I was still bleeding badly from the nose and mouth and noticed abstractly that the mat that I had laid two days ago was flecked and smeared red, and that my ribs hurt like hell.

'Go and rip the tickets for the next house. '

Nausea and imbalance overtook me, and Scourge told me to go and lie down. Later in the evening, feeling something was wrong, I walked back to the tent and opened a flap. When I looked in I

186

saw that a small brawl had broken out in the ring. Mugs were moving out of the crowd to join it. It looked like it would get out of hand, but the showmen miraculously refrained from throwing any punches, giving Michael time to soothe everyone with the right words. But it was close.

'Why didn't you stay with Scourge tearing the tickets?' Michael asked me later that evening as we stood drinking in the Hole in the Wall.

I sipped my beer gingerly because of the cuts in my mouth, pondering my answer. I knew there was still no trust between the two, and I knew I had let him down. I wanted to say I felt crook and thought it best to rest my head because I was worried about my brain, but I knew he wouldn't accept those answers, so all I said was. 'Sorry, mate.'

Michael nodded, and then said, 'Your gloves were too big, a little man can't hurt a big man when he's wearing heavy gloves. Why didn't you punch and move? And why didn't you wear your headgear?'

I didn't answer. How could I explain that I wanted to stand and trade punches with him, to prove something to myself, when I was not even sure what that was? Or worse, admit that I couldn't see half of his big slow punches coming?

The next morning Scourge came to our camp early. 'Haven't you been to bed?' I asked, because I knew Scourge was not an early riser.

He grinned, ran his hand through his hair that hadn't been washed or combed, and we sat in the sun, letting the slowly increasing heat warm us from the inside out.

'Why don't you get that broken tooth fixed?' I said and then I waited a while before asking what I really wanted to know. 'You disappointed in me?' I said it quickly, rubbing a hand over my badly swollen face. Suddenly overtaken by shame.

'Proud of you,' he answered.

'I'll make some coffee,' I said, embarrassedly walking away.

Soon after Michael exploded out of his caravan and came over to join us. We only found out about Bus and Chris when Chippie, coughing, stumbled out of the trailer.

'They left last night.'

'Did Fuggsi run him out?' I asked.

'No, he told us he had a brain tumour. He said the doctor told him if it was hit it could kill him. He told me Michael wouldn't believe him, so he was just going to leave.'

'I don't,' Michael said.

'When did the doctor tell him that, he hasn't had time to see one?' I asked.

'Before he joined us,' Chippie said. 'He told me that he wanted to test out the doctor's theory, that's why he was travelling with us. And then last night while we were sitting around the fire, he said he was going to leave. He talked Chris into going with him. He told him he would only get hurt if he stayed.'

'Why didn't you try and stop him?' Michael asked, squeezing his cup as if he wanted to crush it.

'We did, Michael, all of us.'

Michael nodded, staring at Chippie as if he were trying to make up his mind whether he believed him or not, and then he said in a level, controlled voice, 'They'll never work on the show grounds again.'

Chippie then asked me for fifty cents, and when I wanted to know why, he told me that was the price of a cigarette in the staff canteen.

'What happened to all your money?' I asked, exasperated, but Chippie fell into a violent fit of coughing before he could answer, and when it stopped, he just shrugged his shoulders.

Chris was only a kid, but he didn't have much to go back to. A motel room, no job or family. If he could have stuck it out with Michael he could have made a life on the show grounds. It was a hard life, but it was better than no life. I believed Chris had made a mistake. Bus was much older, too crazy, you couldn't decide for him. Another two good boys gone.

'That just leaves Black Snake, Chippie and Stretch,' Michael said.

'And Fuggsi and Kassi,' Scourge added.

'Fuggsi won't fight, reckons his arm's still hurting. If he doesn't, him and Kassi can clear out, I'm sick of keeping people who won't fight.' We all nodded in agreement.

The rest of the troupe climbed slowly down from the trailer in dribs and drabs, and by the time Fuggsi and Kassi woke, shadows were streaming through the skeleton of the Ferris wheel like elongated maypole banners.

That night Fuggsi fought in the first house, but refused to fight again. I believed his shoulder was hurting him, but Michael would fight with broken arms, and he expected the same from his troupe.

Kassi had to be encouraged to stand on the line-up board. She thrived off Fuggsi's invincibility and when Fuggsi showed weakness, Kassi lost all courage. I felt sorry for her as she stood in front of the crowd with her head lowered. She seemed to be willing herself smaller and more insignificant; a waif with tattooed legs wrapped in a maroon velvet boxing gown. Mercifully, no girl wanted to fight her. I knew that would be the end for both of them.

After we packed up, the three of us wandered again to the Hole in the Wall. The secrecy of its locations never stopped fascinating me. It was like searching for treasure. It could be between the octopus and a shooting gallery, or the haunted house and the dodgem cars. It could be anywhere.

As you drank your beer or rum, you could see big rides hurtling and spinning across the night, hear the whoosh as they displaced air, the screams of kids as they hung on for dear life, but nobody could see or find you. Even Michael had to ask at each new show. 'Where'd they put up the Hole?' I was starting to feel more at home there.

'No, just living money,' Scourge answered me, as we waited for Michael to return with the drinks, gingerly feeling his hand that had remained swollen since the fight in Gin Gin. 'The big towns are no good for us.'

When Michael returned, he said, 'I'm going to tell Fuggsi he has to leave.' We all nodded in agreement. We were drinking rum; it seemed to be an occasion for something a little stronger.

Fuggsi told us himself he was leaving, saving Michael the trouble. They came up to me before they left. Kassi stood close to Fuggsi, smiling up at him seductively, and said to me, 'I want to make a photo of you and Fuggsi.'

Fuggsi stood next to me, dark sunglasses hiding his eyes, wearing an American baseball cap that left the top half of his face in shadow. He was unsmiling.

As we waited for the click of the camera in his eight hundred dollar telephone, he said, 'No white man has ever treated me in my life as good as Michael and you have.'

I looked at him incredulously, thinking that maybe he only wanted to say something nice. But he meant it, I could tell by his sad face.

'I'm going back to get my son out of the institution, Wayne.'

'If they don't let you take him?'

'I don't know yet, I don't know,' he answered, removing his glasses. His eyes I noticed were moving like a man being attacked by five dogs from different directions.

'You got my money, bro?' Black Snake asked as he came over to join us. When I handed him the change, all that was left of a

190

couple of thousand dollars, he said, 'I'll be back, bro, I'll catch up to you in Mareeba.'

I knew he wouldn't return, and I was right. Fuggsi, Kassi and Black Snake left together, and then we were four.

'Let's get this fucking tent down, Stretch, and don't piss around. And get rid of those fuck'n' girls, Chippie, I've told you I don't want them hanging around when we are working.' In our haste a pole fell, narrowly missing my still swollen head.

I drove the two boys to Innisfail. Karla and Mikey rode with their father. We were like a decimated army marching away from a lost battle.

'What's Michael so angry about?' Chippie asked like a kid who'd been belted for something he didn't do.

'Don't know,' I said, but I thought I did. Michael didn't have a real troupe any more. His best fighters had left him. This would never have happened to his pop.

'That fight I had,' I began tentatively, 'I don't want you to feel bad or sorry on my account. I know I let you down a bit, but I did my best.'

'You didn't let us down,' Chippie protested. But I had, and we all knew it.

INNISFAIL

Innisfail was a river town, another cane town.

After the tent was up, we wandered over to the old pub across from the show grounds. We sat around tables in the back bar while the staff, abiding by the unwritten law of showground apartheid, drank noisily in the main bar. Scourge had left Townsville early that morning, and while we were breaking our backs putting up the tent with four men, he had gone river crabbing.

Italians were the backbone of Innisfail. They had come in droves at the turn of the century to cut sugar cane, but Chinese had arrived after the gold had run out on the Palmer River and started banana plantations many years before.

A chinese man scurried from hidden rooms and laid an immense pan of crab in black bean sauce on the table. His wife walked slowly behind him carrying a pan of steaming rice.

Food in the Australian bush hasn't changed for generations. It's bland, overcooked, sustaining. Australian steaks are unsurpassable, but are often served resembling charcoal. We were licking our fingers, sucking at the bones, trying to dislodge another sliver of white meat smothered in delicate foreign tastes, when the boys walked in and told Michael there was no food in camp.

'Eat in the staff canteen and book it up.' It was the only solution, because there was no imagining what either Chippie or Stretch could cook.

Chippie nodded and turned to Stretch. 'Let's get a beer.'

But Michael stopped them. 'Stretch, you get back and fix those fuck'n' side walls. You hung them wrong again. Do it now.' When Stretch began to protest, he yelled, 'Now,' and began to stand.

Even Scourge, whose hierarchical impulses were strong, began to argue tentatively on Stretch's behalf, but left it when he saw Michael's zeal.

'What are we going to do about getting more fighters?' I asked, getting up to buy beers, licking at the crevasses in my hands where sauce may have gathered.

'I got some boys coming tomorrow night to give us a hand,' Michael answered as if nothing had happened.

'What, where did you find them?'

'I went for a drive downtown and saw some Murri fellas walking around. Good boys, I reckon.'

Michael and I left early, leaving Scourge to pay for the feast.

The Murris stood on our line-up board as if they belonged to the tent and had been with us from the beginning. I hoped they would travel with us, but they didn't.

We had three wild houses in a tent packed to the rafters, and could have had four but Michael decided we didn't have enough security. Scourge argued with him because there was good money to be earned, but Michael was right; we didn't have enough boxers to keep things under control. There were no big men to line the side walls and watch for trouble, none to weave through the crowd, ready to have a quick and forceful word with any unruly mugs. And if it went wrong, we only had Chippie and Stretch.

The Aboriginal boys who had come to fight for us couldn't be expected to brawl on our behalf, and the showmen would take the brawl and turn it into a war.

It was a night of rough, dirty fights. Italians always obliged. One white fighter had to be thrown out after kneeing and elbowing his Aboriginal opponent. The crowd started dividing along racial lines. Better to cut the losses and walk.

We ate toasted cheese sandwiches in the staff canteen after closing up the tent. I chewed mine slowly, worrying about the needles and pins that stabbed periodically at my head since my fight, and the feeling that somebody was tightening a clamp above each ear. I pondered on the times I had lost my balance.

'It's hard when you don't have any big blokes. These mugs will always start something when they think they can get away with it. I had to keep talking to them over the microphone, otherwise it would have got out of control. But that doesn't always work.'

'What?' I said, still wrapped up in my own problems, but I heard what he said. I knew that without Mauler, Snake, Bundy, Fuggsi, Leroy and Dennis we were like jugglers without balls.

Next morning we breakfasted on bacon and egg burgers and coffee in the canteen. When Michael told me to do all my eating there, and book it up, I felt like a housewife who had just learned that her husband had hired a maid. I lingered after Michael left, ordering more coffee.

'Chippie fought all right last night.'

'He's getting better,' somebody else said.

'That little Murri fella could fight.'

'Did you see that bastard throw the elbow.'

I twisted around, listening casually to the comments. It was staff and showmen leaning over the tables, hands wrapped around mugs, discussing last night's fights across plates smeared with egg yoke and grease. I hadn't realized how popular the fights were with our own mob.

Chippie and Stretch shuffled in smoking and coughing. Sometimes I wondered whether they ever washed. Their hair was uncombed, their shirts hung loose, their feet were filthy, they seemed to be half asleep. But it didn't matter I supposed, because they had the trailer to themselves now, and the girls still loved them.

'Order what you want,' I said, 'as long as it's only food. You've got to buy your own cigarettes and coke.'

'Too easy,' Stretch said, and then they ordered, and came to sit by me.

'We're leaving this afternoon,' I said, and then I waited with them until their food arrived, trying to avoid their cigarette smoke that floated thickly towards me.

Michael came back to camp just before dark with a small white mini-moke car. Mikey was driving. I knew then that we must have earned well in Innisfail. We left after pulling off its roof and hoisting the car onto the top of the Kenworth with a borrowed forklift.

It was full night as we turned and climbed through the highlands towards Mareeba on the Atherton Tableland, 1000 metres above sea level. Fog filled the hollows, drifting away like pollen as we careened over rises, and then enshrouding us as we dropped down again. Sometimes through the fog and dark you could hear water surging and you understood that it must be falling from great heights, but from where exactly remained a secret.

MAREEBA

Mareeba rodeo was one of the biggest in the country. When we woke next morning, we found ourselves surrounded by the tents of hundreds of rodeo aficionados. It was afternoon before our own tent was standing, but long before the banners and flags were flying, Aboriginals wandered over in curious, excited groups.

Michael's tent had always attracted Aboriginals. Historically they had always been the backbone of the business, the grist to the mill. The fighting seemed to come naturally and the rough travelling was second nature. It seemed to me that although some of the young men had never even seen a boxing tent before, it was as if they understood that it was their theatre. That it was here that they would be respected and heralded. That it belonged to them more than to any other.

They were darker, a third darker than Leroy, twice as dark as Mauler, and they brought with them boxing skills that I hadn't seen on the whole run. Deft head movements, fast, skilled hands, explosions of power, a good nature. It was a pleasure to see the pleasure in the fight.

It was a night of pot-pourri. A big, confident cowgirl, wearing a black, scuffed, bull rider's hat, and with a broken middle front tooth not unlike Scourge's, wandered into camp and offered to fight for us. Michael matched her against a tall, disarmingly pretty girl, who put up her hand clearly but tentatively. I spoke to the girl before the fight, and her placidity and urbaneness concerned me.

The girl, who gave as good as she got against the cowgirl, was cheered on by a concerned but proud mother and father, and an excited younger sister in loud, civil language. Disgracefully, I wondered how an Aboriginal family could be so normal.

A man who had toured years before with Michael on his trips through the missions turned up wanting to fight. He was staggering drunk and not as young as he used to be, but forbidding him was like keeping a starving dog from food. He threw punches until his legs buckled, and then threw more from his knees.

After the fight, he sat on the ground hugging his opponent, breathing painfully, blood dribbling from his nose, one eye swelling and closing slowly. Sweat reeking of cheap wine ran shimmering across his chest and over his belly, as if he sat out in a tropical downpour. Michael gave him a hug when he paid him and then he left forgetting the flagon of wine he had given me to look after.

'Get my son out of there, you bastards. You fuck'n' cunts, he's only sixteen.'

'The boy he's fighting is only sixteen,' I said to the woman who was standing at the tent entrance. 'He won't get hurt, but go and get him yourself if you want.' The boy, whose blond hair made it hard to tell him apart from Chippie when they clinched, refused to stop fighting. The woman walked back to me and began swearing anew.

'Piss off, ya stupid bitch,' I finally said in frustration, and then she walked off.

'Fuck'n' mongrels, I hope you cunts die,' were the last words she said to us.

197

The cowboys stayed away. I could hear their yahoos around the rodeo ring and the intoxicated, high-spirited ode to brotherhood at the bar which was only rock-throwing distance from the boxing tent, but they never wandered down. We had to pull apart two Aboriginal girls who were tearing at each other's hair and dresses, before we could finally close up the tent for the night and wander up to the bar where a band was setting out their instruments.

Sipping my first rum, I heard the announcement that the rodeo was finished for the evening. The crowd began to swell around the bar, in front of the band. The boys began with rock and roll: Credence, the Doobies, the Eagles, all played loudly, perfectly, flooding me with the sensations of a youthful, hope-filled time.

Michael, Scourge and myself stood in a circle sipping our rums, saying nothing important, letting it burn our insides, tricking the important part of our guts into believing we were warm when we were freezing in the high plateau night. Moving parts of our bodies clandestinely to the beat, because tough men don't dance.

After the third rum, the music slowed and the words became clearer. Aboriginal grievances making up the song text. The crowd that was a harmonious black and white mixture, seemed to know all the words.

Michael had bought many rums for an old Aboriginal man who had promised to find fighters to travel with us, before he told him to stop bludging. I was surprised at Michael's rough rebuff, because I knew how well he understood Aboriginal drinking culture. But I was also astonished at the indignant reaction of the old man. At his menace of violence.

He called over his nephew who was enormous and drunk, and together they threatened to bash us with eighty fighters.

'How many can you put together?' the nephew asked confidently, swaying like a bull elephant.

'Fifty men,' Michael said, not wanting to back down. I wondered where all the fighters would come from, since the bulk of the rides and joints were in Cairns, but quietly sipped my drink, supporting his bluff.

It was solved peacefully, but not before the old man threatened us a number of times more with his mob. It was a serious menace and it underlined the man's sense of insult. Something Michael underestimated.

Dennis and I would sometimes go for a beer, and when we did, although I often offered to shout, he always insisted on paying his way. He knew about cultural misunderstandings and what the consequences could be.

A copper, who was one of many standing around ready to enforce the peace, walked over to speak to us when the Murris left.

'He's a tribal leader,' the policeman said, 'and he's telling you the truth when he said he could put a big mob together.'

'What about this nephew?' Michael asked.

'A bad bastard, pity you didn't give him a hiding,'

The band, who stood in front of an enormous Aboriginal flag, played with passion and delight until the early hours, and when we woke next day, I could hear the loudspeakers announcing the start of the bareback.

A bareback rider locks a hand tightly under something called the 'suitcase handle', binding himself to the horse as tightly as Chinese women wrapped their feet before the arrival of the communists. It gives you the best chance of staying on, but it can also tie you up.

The Murri cowboy who was thrown, and whose hand caught under the suitcase handle, was paunchy. I thought that would be a disadvantage as he was forced to run alongside the galloping horse to save from being dragged, but he kept up until two pick-up riders rode up beside the horse, shunting it between them.

While one reached for the head stall to slow the horse's gallop, the other tried frantically to reef the rider's hand from the suitcase handle. It took them fifty metres and when the rider ran free, he shook his injured wrist to bring back the blood, and with his good hand waved jauntily to the crowd.

One of the horsemen reached under the buck-jumper and un-singed a strap. Untormented and riderless, the horse became calm. Unlike the bulls I had seen in Rockhampton, the horse had no need for revenge, no yearn to crush or gore.

When I drove out of the gates and headed down the mountain towards Cairns, I was wearing a straw cowboy hat, thinking I could ride any horse or bull myself.

CAIRNS

Michael radioed me to pick up two hitchhikers he'd passed on the road. Aboriginals, with Island blood.

'You want to earn some money,' I asked them after they settled their heavy frames into the car.

'Yeah,' they answered, suspiciously. Both agreed to come and fight for us, but they never showed.

When we unloaded in Cairns, Stretch and Chippie suffered under a hail of abuse from Michael. Any small mistake making him angry.

After the tent was standing, Michael and I went for a drive into town, pulling up beside any Murri we spotted, and asking them if they wanted to fight.

We dropped washing off at a laundry, because our machine had rattled to death, and then Michael walked into a jewellery store and asked them to show him gold chains, because he wanted to buy a present for Mandy. When he came back outside he was furious.

'They told me they didn't have any gold chains, but they were lying. They didn't want to show me any because I'm black. They don't trust me.' Again I didn't believe him, but Michael came up with a plan to prove it.

I was nervous when I walked into the shop because I had never felt comfortable in places that sold expensive trinkets. It was something to do with the arrogance that many salespersons seem to acquire when selling something they can't afford themselves, and because I came from stock that didn't wear glitter.

When I asked for gold chains, trays full were placed on the counter. Michael stood in the doorway, filling it, looking more menacing than I'd ever seen him. He smiled when I told the woman to keep it. 'I don't buy from bigots.'

'I wouldn't have believed it,' I said outside the shop.

'It happens a lot to me,' he replied pulling roughly at his tail.

Our last stop was a fabric shop. Michael wanted new boxing apparel. He ordered yellow and red satin gowns with white piping, and matching white-fringed trunks, a leopard-skin caveman cape with matching trunks, and a sexy fringed leather get-up for any woman boxer who might want to join us.

It was the end of the school holidays, and along with the other show-ground teenagers, Karla and Mikey flew back home the day after we arrived in Cairns. Michael wanted Mikey to stay, but he had had enough.

Mikey hadn't fought since Rockhampton and, since then, had spent most of his time with his uncle, away from the tent. I couldn't blame him, it was rough living in our camp: the food was irregular; we had few amenities, and standing on the line-up board must have been nerve-racking for a twelve year old. Even if he was Michael's boy.

With the departure of Karla, Michael decided to take full control of the finances. He put me in charge of selling tickets, paying the fighters, and being accountable for the night's earnings. For the first time on the trip, I was cut off from the fights, isolated from everything but the roar of the crowd.

Men and boys turned up to box for us on that first night like ants to sugar. Some were the men Michael had stopped on the roads, others just seemed to know they would be needed.

When I handed out the new trunks and gowns, the fighters pawed the fabric, held them to the light to play with the sheen. Modelled them for each other, twisting and posing like catwalk girls, and before my work began, I stood amongst the crowd, admiring the fighters that paraded like menacing dandies under the line-up board lights.

It took a few sessions on the first night before my ticket sales became smooth. Leanne showed me to how to order the bank notes and keep separate denominations in different sections of the money bag, and to hold enough notes in my hand to make faster change.

On the second night, one of Bronco Johnson's sons walked into camp. His colour was one of those startling rich shades you get when the balance of black and white is perfect. His face, unlike his father's crushed and ruined appearance, was unmarked. He arrived unannounced and without celebration; his politeness was disarming.

The man fought with exceptional elegance and only sufficient power and aggression, never once overtaxing himself. It was like watching a cat playfully paw a ball of thread. He left quietly, almost secretively. And then he came back the next night and did the same.

It began to rain steadily on the fourth day, the crowds dwindled, and in the evening I worked alone. When the customers diminished, I moved to the curtain covering the entrance, and peeked inside. It was a mistake. Michael saw me arguing with three men who were trying to bully their way past without paying. They left, but they might not have.

'You don't stand in front of the curtain, you stand out front. If they reach the curtain, you'll always have trouble keeping them out. Stand out the front.'

Later, I went to pay the fighters. A man who resembled a small Mike Tyson immediately came to where I was standing, asking, 'Hey bro, do I get thirty or fifty dollars?' He kept repeating it, encouraging all the other fighters to crowd around and ask the same.

'I told you one at a time,' Michael said to me when he saw that I was having trouble.

'I'm doing my best, mate,' I answered, frantically trying to check the fighters' names against a list I had made.

'Just walk away from them,' Michael said. I did, but they followed. It was then I noticed Michael swearing and shaking his head.

At the end of the evening, he yelled again, 'Chippie, you and Stretch collect all the gear, and make sure nothing goes missing, otherwise I'll fucking kill you.'

On the last night of the show, there was a small brawl inside the tent. I didn't even know it was going on. Later Michael told me that one of the boxers fighting for the tent had joined in. Cairns was a gang town.

That night Michael and I walked back to camp together. Michael heard that there was trouble on the grounds, and the night's takings were several thousands of dollars. I carried it under my jacket, my arm wrapped tightly around my chest as if it were broken. Michael walked close to me, hiding the bulge with his bulk.

We were forced to walk close to the fight, but it was hard to tell how many were involved. It could have been ten or a hundred. When we got back to the caravan, Michael waited for a phone call. They always called him when there was trouble. When there were bad boys in town.

When no phone call came, we walked towards the Hole in the Wall, and heard from other showmen that the fight had only been between a few mugs. The crowd that had gathered around the trouble was just show-ground flotsam and jetsam that had been sucked up by the storm.

The Hole in the Wall had been erected at an unusual location. It was protected from the back by a wide, deep storm drain, but its entrance was unnaturally exposed to any public who wandered through the back reaches of the show ground.

The woman who strolled past twice was tall and good-looking, but when she came further into the bar light, you could see marks of life deeply etched around her eyes and mouth.

The showman who called her in to have a drink was married. They were just talking, drinking and laughing. It was only when they started dancing that the trouble started.

That night there was an unusual abundance of showwomen in the Hole. They huddled together like an undisciplined rugby pack, brightening up the normally dour atmosphere with feminine sounds and movements. At a certain time, it became clear they were discussing the woman.

They began by verbally abusing her, and only much later, after the woman refused to be intimidated and leave, did they physically attack her. There were five of them, but the stranger fought back against the biting, scratching, hair pulling, punches and kicks.

The woman was saved by her dance partner, who pulled her attackers away and walked her to safety, but not before having to duck a chair that was hurled at him by one of the showwomen.

There had been nothing going on, it had only been a flirt, and I didn't understand why they were so violent towards her. It wasn't their husband she was dancing with.

I had always considered Aaron's sister Shelly the most steadfast of people. My only home-cooked meals on the whole run were served by her, and I was never made unwelcome in her camp. Nobody was.

'I would have done the same thing,' she said to me the following day, as we watched her husband coach his horse over a fence that reached to the animal's forehead. He was competing in the high jump, the gala event on the show-jumpers' circuit. The riders were expected to jump their horses higher and higher until a winner was left standing.

'But it would have had nothing to do with you,' I countered, completely taken by surprise. 'Why would you want to get involved?'

Shelly had married outside the showman's guild, almost tantamount to a Muslim marrying a Christian, but she was a showgirl from blood and heart, and there was no one who would defend the lifestyle more fiercely. 'He's a married man,' she said.

Shelly's husband flew over his horse's head, landing in a bath of sawdust. The height of the fence had been raised to two metres.

'We work as teams on the show grounds. Without the men a lot of the women would be out of business. We can't let outsiders take them, this is the only life we know.' She laughed wildly as her husband shook himself like a wet dog, spraying sawdust over his startled horse that he still held tightly by the reins.

'The men have got to know we won't accept that sort of

behaviour,' she said, smiling again. 'But most of them know that already.'

In Cairns, only hours before we started our trip south to Tully, I learned through one of my periodic emails to my wife that my Amsterdam life and Estonian business needed urgent attention. This time I couldn't ignore it.

'I have to get back to Europe,' I told Michael when I returned from the internet office.

'Trouble?' he asked, and it was then I noticed his new gold tooth.

'I got to take care of things,' I said honestly.

'All right, take the car.'

'Thanks, you won't need it?'

'No,' he said. 'Run's almost over.'

'Tooth looks good.'

TULLY

It seemed like an eternity until the heavily laden cane train rolling slowly forward on the narrow-gauge tracks passed in front of us. The long line of trucks and cars strung out on both sides of the road waited patiently, understanding that the area's commerce took priority.

Stretch's new girlfriend rode in the front seat next to me, her dress folded to her thighs. As the heat in the stationary car became more unbearable, she began to lift the hem of her dress with underhanded flicks of her fingers, disturbing the air, creating the smallest of breezes, cooling her crotch.

Chippie and Stretch smoked on the back seat, as far apart as possible, each gazing steadfastly at the small train carriages that were hauled along tail to tail like a line of baby elephants, both intent on not passing under the gaze of the other. The boys had been arguing for days.

An Aboriginal couple road with Michael in the Kenworth. The man who Michael had named Super Murri, had proved a good fighter and a willing traveller. His girlfriend who was silent and friendly had, without being asked, started cooking and cleaning for us.

Tully was built in the shadows of high green mountains, part of the Great Dividing Range that hugged the coast in this part of Australia. Clouds lay on the ridges and filled the canyons of the mountains softening the looming green mass like a crochet shawl laid across a severely cut bodice.

The town had a couple of pubs, a bank, the odds and ends of small commerce, and at the end of the main street, a cane crushing factory with two chimneys that belched out steam like the stacks of an ocean liner that had lost its way and found itself sailing on lawn amongst palm trees.

It was old-fashioned, peaceful, a place where your children could roam without fear. Ten years before the showmen had to battle a hundred mugs along its main street.

'What's the problem with them two?' Michael asked me after he had told Stretch and Chippie to shut up their fucking arguing when we were putting up the tent.

'The girl. Chippie reckons she's a slut. He keeps telling Stretch she's just using him.'

'Is she?'

'I don't know,' I answered, ' but I don't think she's a settling type of girl. One thing I do know, Stretch is head over heels for her.'

After the tent was up, Stretch told Michael he wanted to leave.

'You fuck'n leave me,' he told him, 'and you'll never work on the show grounds again. And neither will your girlfriend.'

Michael's patience had become limited and selective since the last of the Murris had left us. More and more often as the trip went on, he had become tyrannical.

'Did you write down the local boy's name?' Michael asked, after the first fight had began.

'Yeah,' I yelled up to him, louder than necessary, frustrated that I was being checked like a school kid.

'Stand in the corner to pay the fucking fighters, and pay them one at a time,' Michael said to me after the first house had finished.

'I'm doing that,' I yelled back.

'You're not fucking doing that.'

'Pay them your fucking self,' I finally said, handing him the money bag. 'I'm finished.'

Scourge followed me out into the hurly-burly of the night, calling after me, but giving up when I kept moving towards the bar.

When I walked back in before the start of the second session, Michael said smiling, 'I knew you would be back.'

'Give me the money bag,' I said.

'Scourge wanted to do the tickets,' Michael said, 'but I knew you would be back.'

Michael challenged a monster in the last house of the night. 'You're gunna have to fight me, is that all right with you?' he said to the local fellow who stood towering over him on the line-up board, a bemused look on his broad brown face.

When Michael whistled, Chippie began to beat the drum while Stretch shook the bell, each coaxing an unnatural cacophony out of their instruments. Both trying to drown the other out.

The local man who outweighed Michael by forty kilos flew at him, throwing punches that could drop a bullock, but Michael knew how to fight monsters and swayed and hooked him into submission.

After we had packed up, Michael wanted to have a drink, but I declined, it wasn't the time to be drinking together. He rubbed his arm that he had hurt in the fight, and walked away.

The next morning, just after daylight, Michael and I drove to the main street to buy pies for breakfast. It was a Sunday, God's day, and Tully was still closed down. It made me think back to my youth, to the heinous time when even the pubs were forced to stay shut on Sundays. Fortunately, even in those dark days, bakers and paper shops were exempt.

We were standing outside the pie shop on a street that ran down from the mountains with a determined slant; I was standing on the upper side. The pies wafted a pepper, meaty fragrance. Their heat steaming the paper bag that they came in until it became wet and soft. It was a clear crisp morning, one that made you glad to be alive.

In the certainty that I'd been wronged, I was still angry. Perhaps it was the slant of the road that made Michael's size less daunting, or sometimes dogs just need to bark.

'I've fucking done everything for you,' I said. 'I've done it as well as I could. You had no right to speak to me like that.'

I swore some more, pointing out how he would have been fucked without me. I went further than he normally allowed people to go, crossed a line that was forbidden to most people. But he gave me more room, and I used it.

'You don't treat me like a bastard,' I finally said, ready to fight. 'You yell at the other blokes that don't give a fuck, not at me.' I let the pie bag fall to my side, ready to drop cleanly, freeing my hands.

Michael's face told me he'd reached the point where he couldn't turn back, his pride wouldn't let him. It was time to give me a bashing. But today, I didn't care. Today, I thought, is a good day to die.

A single word, a drop of a shoulder, the smell of hot fresh baked pies, a glance that reminds you a mate is standing in front of you. That's how close it comes sometimes.

I liked few men I'd met as well as Michael, I respected him, and his troupe had come to mean as much to me as it did for him. That's why I stayed mad for so long.

*

211

That evening, I had my last drink with the showmen. The staff were drinking in the back bar, but you only realized who was out there when one put his or her face to the metre-square window that had been cut in a partitioning wall to order a drink. The pool table and dartboard were in the staff section.

'Super Murri wants to leave,' Michael said to me, as we ordered our first beer. I could tell by the way Michael held his left arm across his chest that it was still giving him trouble.

'Why?' I asked.

'He reckons his girl's playing around.'

'It's in his head,' I said, 'I've never met a sweeter, more loyal woman.'

'I know,' Michael answered.

'Will you be all right?' I asked.

Michael looked insulted, but then said, 'It's only a few more shows, we'll make out.'

It was a big drink that night because there was a lot of people to say goodbye to. Before we left the pub, Michael bought every cigar in the place and gave them to me.

'For the trip back,' he said as he handed them to me, and then he asked me to take the caravan back to Tullamore.

'Won't you need it?' I asked, only mildly surprised, because you never really knew what Michael would do.

'No, I'll sleep in the Kenworth hotel, your old room,' he added grinning under the street lamp that made his new gold tooth gleam and the others fade away as if they were white sheets hanging out to dry.

'I'll get Mandy to run me into Dubbo, and catch the bus back to Cessnock when I get there,' I said, remembering drunkenly that at Tullamore I wouldn't have my own transport.

'No,' Michael said again, 'keep the car, it's yours.'

Before I left the next morning, I walked slowly through

212

sideshow alley. It had rained in the night, and streams of water lay in front of the joints along both sides.

It'll be dry before too long, I thought to myself, breathing in the cool, wet, earthy air, feeling the sun that had just risen hit the back of my neck, realizing that it was already sucking at the water.

I stopped when I came to the boxing tent, climbed the ladder and sat on the line-up board, waving my feet over the edge, looking left and right down the alley. The joints and rides were in shadow, their jumble of bright colours softened. There were no people, no noise.

Soon the sun would lift higher and bake the colours hard; the generators would start up; the music would be turned to full volume. The mugs would arrive.

As I drove out of the grounds, I looked momentarily in the rear-vision mirror, checking that the caravan was following, and then I glanced into the side mirror. The Ferris wheel, perfectly round and stark against the faded sky, stood steadfast.

When I heard Michael's sharp whistle, I leaned out of the window and waved a last goodbye to the group who had gathered, and then it was just the road ahead.

HOME

I drove south back along the coast highway, and turned west at Townsville, heading into the bush along the Flinders highway. A better way home Michael reckoned. The road was almost straight, but it climbed and at times the old Ford slowed badly. At Charters Towers, I stopped to fill up the tank and buy food, coughing repeatedly in the dry burnt air.

'You come up from the coast, mate?' a grease-smudged man with heavily haired forearms asked me as he finished pumping my petrol. I coughed again and nodded.

'That's what's up with you. None of that wet air up here. But you'll be all right in a bit,' he added unsmiling. And then he said as if he knew I was one of those blokes who had to be reminded. 'Watch for roos if you plan on travelling at night.'

I headed southeast out of Charters Towers and followed a road that alternated from one to two lanes and back to one again without any discernible pattern. When the road-trains tore past on the one-lane sections, I was pushed over to the side, buffeted by wind and showered with dirt and stones, but there was nothing to do, they were the kings of the road.

Two hours out of Charters, just before the light gave completely

214

away, I pulled off the road, lit a fire and boiled some tea water. It was a clear star-filled night, and no punishment sitting alone, smoking a cigar, drinking sweet black tea, watching my fire flicker, gazing into the blackness beyond it, and knowing you were miles from anywhere.

Just before light, I tore off, anxious to get some distance behind me, and feeling a bit silly for letting the kangaroos frighten me off the roads.

I filled up in Clermont, and drove straight through Emerald. It was in Roma that they started warning me about the roos again.

It was nearing midnight when I lay my swag on the back seat of the Ford, and crawled underneath its flaps. A light rain was drumming soothingly on the car roof. When I awoke it was still dark and wet. I drove slowly back onto the narrow road, and steadily increased my speed, peering periodically into the dark at the edge of my lights.

I braked heavily when I saw the first roo, skidding badly, the weight of the caravan pushing me forward and sideways. When my front bumper bar drove into the roo, I felt the manifest thump of collision with living flesh, and then I heard the meaty knocks as my car rolled over the body. I drove on relieved that the Ford was undamaged, and then I saw the second roo.

It was much larger than the first, and came bounding directly towards the car with a suicidal commitment. It was as if the roo had made a pact that for the grazing rights to fenceless green paddocks dotted with stands of shady eucalyptus, clear running water, all the does he could mount, he would give his life.

Just before his death, I could see him clearly in my headlights. His eyes were wide open, unmoving, glazed. There didn't seem to be any panic, only that he held his head at a crooked angle as if he wanted to get a better look at his slayer.

The thump of the roo's body against the Ford was much louder than the collision with the first animal. It lifted onto and over the bonnet, sliding across the front windscreen before it fell broken into the darkness.

A few hundred metres down the road, the heat indicator in the Ford showed red, the car began to wheeze, and then to slow. When I got out and checked the front with a flashlight, steam was rising out of the cracked radiator, the grille was shattered, the bonnet bent, and the right-hand light broken and dangling from its electric cable like a garrotted rabbit left hanging on a fence post.

I swore violently, but without passion. I had grown used to problems travelling with the tent, and I knew they would get solved. I slid back onto the front seat of my car, and rifled through my bag, pulling out one of Michael's cigars. I reckoned that I was halfway between Surat and Saint-George; that would put me about sixty miles away from help. I lit the cigar and puffed, wrapped myself in my swag and waited for a passing vehicle.

I was fifty years old, I contemplated, as I gazed out into the black drizzle, through the window clouded grey with cigar smoke, and although I'd lost seven or eight pounds, I had never felt fitter, never happier.

I'd come back searching for a place, my people, and I'd found them. I had in the past always left Australia feeling that I didn't belong. The life of my old mates had become too different. They were family men, some had become grandfathers. They lived a sedentary, habitual life. A good fulfilling one. But not mine!

On the show ground, there were no settlers. People danced through the day to the rhythms of an erratic piper. It was the regularity that frightened me: like a layer of coal dust settling on your lungs day after day, until you can't breath any more.

I dozed then, waking startled when a road-train roar passed, rocking the car. I could only see its lights as it raced away in the dark, but I swore at it anyway. I was still unnerved as I relit my cigar and settled back under my swag.

Wish the boys were here, I thought, as I looked out into the sky that was showing the first subtle signs of day and, at first indistinctly and then lucidly, a parade of dark faces moved across my imagination like a subconscious roll-call of indigenous tent fighters, and I found myself pondering on small incidents, recalling details; smiling and shaking my head in astonishment at the passion and whimsy of their lives.

I wondered vaguely if Bus's tumour was still a problem, and if Chris had found a home. I worried that Chippie and Stretch would leave Michael before the end of the run because then he wouldn't have anybody, and neither would they.

Three more road-trains sped dangerously past, but I didn't care. I was in no hurry, somebody would stop, and when they did, my travels with men would be over.

Amsterdam

My gratitude to my countryman and fellow writer, David Colmer, for his encouragement and support in writing this book.

Australia

I owe many thanks to the following members of the showmen's guild who welcomed me into their unique and sublimely non-conformist world. They fed me, guided and befriended me: John Castles, John Davis, Ron and Shelley Easy, Peter and Margo Gill, Jason Gill, John and Joan Godfrey, Bob Martin, Richard and Janet Miller, Darren and Kathleen Miller, Jamie Pickett, Charlie Pink, Aaron and Sharon Pink, John Short, Jay Short.

And my sincere gratitude to all the other guild members, without whom this book would not have been possible.

Thank you also to: Shaky, Balls, and Harry Houdini (Frankie), three showground characters among many.

I will never forget the friendliness shown me on my travels by Boss and Allene O'Bryan, Leo and Joyce Pietsch, and Mark and Janine Phillips.

Nor the fighters who afforded me the opportunity to travel with men. Dennis Cutmore, Tuffie, Brendan Prince, Kevin Pitt, Adrian Dominic, Black Snake, (Jason) Fuggsi, Kassi, Chippie, Stretch, Zac, Chris (Cherbourg), Bus, Chris (Proserpine), Super Murri, Aaron Pink.

Above all, I am indebted to the Karaitiana family.

Firstly to Steven and Gita Karaitiana for their warm welcome and recollections. And especially to Michael and Samantha (Mandy) Joy

Karaitiana, and to their children Karla, Mikey, Marshall, Gracie, and Sasha. This last great tent boxing family accepted me in their midst and gave me their trust unconditionally.

Great forefathers held this story together like a binding of gold thread: Roy Bell and Rehita Lester Karaitiana. Lest we forget!